To Mary
one of the family

with
we

Christmas 2009

KIN

Scottish poems about family

KIN

Scottish poems about family

———————————

Edited with an introduction by
HAMISH WHYTE

SCOTTISH POETRY LIBRARY
By leaves we live

Polygon

For my mother Alicia Whyte (née Berry)

First published in 2009 by
The Scottish Poetry Library
5 Crichton's Close
Edinburgh EH8 8DT
In association with
POLYGON

Introduction copyright © 2009 Hamish Whyte
Selection copyright © 2009 Scottish Poetry Library
Individual poems © see *Acknowledgements*

ISBN 978 1 84697 103 7

The publishers acknowledge support from
the Scottish Arts Council and the Russell Trust
towards the publication of this title

Scottish
Arts Council

Typeset in Great Britain by Antony Gray
Printed and bound in Sweden by Scandbook.

CONTENTS

MOTHERS

FATHERS

Editor's note: Glossing of words has been kept to the end of each poem.

INTRODUCTION

The BBC TV programme asks the question 'Who do you think you are?' and seeks answers by following various celebrities up their family trees. They all seem to think that their forebears have some influence on them, whether through genes or some more esoteric osmosis. 'That's why I love the sea!' they exclaim. 'Because great-grandpa was a sailor!'

We all do this to a certain degree. As a child I was told by my mother that I had my grandmother's feet. Somehow we seem more inclined to see ourselves reflected in other family members than thinking we're just ourselves: we like to find out 'how we got here'. We all want to belong and family is an easy way to do this – though not always so easy.

In a supposedly disintegrating society, and presumably because of that perception, the notion of family is trumpeted daily – by politicians, by the soaps (notably *EastEnders*), by the media. And of course, family has always made good drama, from *Oedipus* to *The Three Sisters*. It's the perfect dynamic: clash of generation and gender.

Are Scottish families any different from any others? In essence, surely not; though some would argue that the idea of family – of cohesion, of loyalty – is stronger in Scotland. Certainly the myth of the clan still holds sway.

In Scottish literature the family ideal is most famously represented in Robert Burns's 'The Cotter's Saturday Night'. This poem has divided the critics. The main charge against is that it sentimentalised real life and work. It's sentimental, yes, but still paints a realistic picture of life on the land in late eighteenth-century Scotland – Burns was a cotter himself.

The poem has certainly cast a long shadow over Scottish literature's portrayal of family life, both for bad – the couthie excesses of Whistlebinkie and the Kailyard – and good: poems such as Alexander Anderson's 'Cuddle Doon' may be cosy but it's a real, recognisable family situation he depicts. Stewart Conn's twentieth-century Todd is a direct descendant of the Cotter and his family bible, 'in the kitchen, over porridge and cream / his talk all of Jacob, of Moses . . . ' and surely Kathleen Jamie's 'Crystal Set', with the family cosily gathered round the radio, is not too far away?

'The Cotter's Saturday Night' is a more domestic version of Burns's 'A Man's A Man'. 'From Scenes like these, old SCOTIA'S grandeur springs': Burns is saying that it's these ordinary folk – the farm worker, his family and friends, their life of hard work and simple pleasures – who give the nation its strength, not the doings of kings and lords – the democratic concept of the virtues of sense and worth.

Burns's model for the poem was Robert Fergusson's earlier 'The Farmer's Ingle', a less pretentious, though still idealised picture of farm life – but Fergusson lets the picture tell the story, undiluted by English, without Burns's portentous moralising or the religious element. The influence of both poems can be seen in 'The Weaver's Saturday' of 1838 – an urban version, with deliberate political colouring.

If 'The Cotter's Saturday Night' features the most functional family in Scottish literature, then the ballad 'Edward, Edward' contains what must be the most dysfunctional: a family destroyed by the son at the instigation of his Lady Macbeth-ish mother. There are plenty of other uncouthie examples, particularly in nineteenth- and twentieth-century literature, with the downside of industrialisation – bad housing, low wages, poverty, alcoholism – reflected in poems, from Janet Hamilton's 'The Drunkard's Wife' to Brian McCabe's 'there was a bottle with a dream in it' ('The Big Sister Poems').

Kin is not intended as any kind of social history of the family in Scotland – that has still to be written. Poets write as they find and readers glean the history as they can. The family does provide almost limitless permutations and situations of emotional and social relationships, whether it's mothers writing about daughters, sisters about brothers, sons about fathers, cousins about cousins – not to mention more distant relations, the ancestors (the family history industry is brilliantly sent up in Hugh McMillan's 'The World Book of the McMillans').

I hope the poems reflect the ordinary ups and downs of family life as well the extremes: poems such as Bill Herbert's 'The

Harvest in March', which captures that moment when a couple becomes a family; Stevenson's 'The Land of Story-Books' which beautifully describes the child apart from its parents making its own world; or the wry mixture of nostalgia and awkward reality in Stewart Conn's filial 'Family Visit'.

One Scottish poet who, perhaps more than any other, has written about the contemporary family is Jackie Kay. Not content with exploring her own family – in moving, affectionate, dramatic and funny poems based on her adoption, her growing up in Scotland as a black woman, her adoptive parents, her meeting with her birth father – she has been bringing out a series of poems exploring the Scottish psyche using the most archetypical family since the cotter's, the Broons (see 'Maw Broon Visits a Therapist' from *Off Colour*).

The anthology is divided into sections, for ease of reference: first of all, a more general one, dealing with families as such (that is, usually a group – parent or parents with children), then sections devoted to particular members of the family: mothers, daughters, brothers, cousins *et al*. After 'Edward' mothers get a better press from their children, both sons and daughters. Interestingly, most of the fathers I've been able to find are seen from a son's rather than a daughter's perspective, and it's the father/son relationship that seems to be the most troubling. There seem to be very few poems by mothers about sons.

Links and echoes between poems will be caught by readers as

they dip in and out of the anthology – for example, the echo of Muir's 'Childhood' I detect in Don Paterson's 'The Thread'; and new ballad (Helen Adam's 'Counting Out Rhyme') harking back to old ballad ('Edward, Edward'). There are also contrasts, like the nice one between Burns's and Hogg's attitude to their daughters, affectionate in their different ways.

Apart from a few examples of poets writing generally (Edwin Muir for one), in poems about family members the poets are most obviously themselves – less easy here to hide behind a persona. The I is I. And writing about one's mother or father is to write about oneself, so there are always at least two people in the poem. We see ourselves in our family and our family in ourselves. Poems, like families, should encompass dialogue, communication – communion even. Every family and every poem is different , in its own way.

Hamish Whyte
March 2009

EDITOR'S ACKNOWLEDGEMENTS

I should like to thank all those who helped this collection along, with suggestions or encouragement, especially Ian Campbell, Gerry Carruthers, Stewart Conn, Lilias Fraser, Diana Hendry, Jim McGonigal, Lizzie MacGregor, Robyn Marsack, Neville Moir and Alison Rae.

HW

Edward, Edward

'Why dois your brand sae drap wi bluid
      Edward, Edward,
Why dois your brand sae drap wi bluid,
   And why sae sad gang yee O?'
'O I hae killed my hauke sae guid,
      Mither, mither,
O I hae killed my hauke sae guid,
   And I had nae mair bot hee O.'

'Your haukis bluid was nevir sae reid,
      Edward, Edward,
Your haukis bluid was nevir sae reid,
   My deir son I tell thee O.'
'O I hae killed my reid-roan steid,
      Mither, mither,
O I hae killed my reid-roan steid,
   That erst was sae fair and frie O.'

'Your steid was auld, and ye hae gat mair,
      Edward, Edward,
Your steid was auld, and ye hae gat mair,
   Sum other dule ye drie O.'
'O I hae killed my fadir deir,
      Mither, mither,
O I hae killed my fadir deir,
   Alas, and wae is mee O!'

'And whatten penance wul ye drie for that,
            Edward, Edward?
And whatten penance wul ye drie for that?
      My deir son, now tell me O.'
'Ile set my feit in yonder boat,
            Mither, mither,
Ile set my feit in yonder boat,
      And Ile fare ovir the sea O.'

'And what wul ye doe wi your towirs and your ha,
            Edward, Edward?
And what wul ye doe wi your towirs and your ha,
      That were sae fair to see O?'
'Ile let thame stand tul they doun fa,
            Mither, mither,
Ile let thame stand tul they doun fa,
      For here nevir mair maun I be O.'

'And what wul ye leive to your bairns and your wife,
            Edward, Edward?
And what wul ye leive to your bairns and your wife,
      Whan ye gang ovir the sea O?'
'The warldis room, late them beg thrae life,
            Mither, mither,
The warldis room, late them beg thrae life,
      For thame nevir mair wul I see O.'

'And what wul ye leive to your ain mither deir,
            Edward, Edward?

And what wul ye leive to your ain mither deir?
    My deir son, now tell me O.'
'The curse of hell frae me sall ye beir,
      Mither, mither,
The curse of hell frae me sall ye beir,
    Sic counseils ye gave to me O.'

ANONYMOUS

brand – sword; *dule* – sorrow; *drie* – endure

from **The Weaver's Saturday**

The weaver and his family take the road,
    Refreshed and happy, frisky, blythe wi' fun,
At sober eve they reach their sweet abode,
    And there the frying-pan begins to croon,
Clad with fresh herring landed from Lochfyne,
    Well spiced and sappy for a hungry gab,
The bonny tea-cups on the table shine;
    And Robin, on his chair, like any nab
    Beside his wife and bairns, brags o'er his promised web.

God's blessing sought with reverence, they begin,
    Nor fash with gentle ceremonious airs,
The happy children sit with merry din
    Around the table and partake their shares.
Then Robin hums the patriarchal grace,
    And thanks the Lord for all his mercies great,
Imploring him to guard the rising race
    From secret snares, that youthful life await,
    And aye prepared for death, their only certain fate.

The dressing pot's hung o'er the glowing fire,
    And cautious heated till it slowly boil,
And friendly shopmates kindly help to stir;
    And Robin, grateful for their gen'rous toil,
Tells glorious news, how commerce through the gloom,
    Blinks like a star on Britain's happy isle,
And muslin weavers, pining at the loom,

Shall yet have some reward for weary toil;
   A *farthing* on the ell can make the weaver smile.

Each stirs awhile aboon the vivid lowe,
   And sweat is trickling down their beards like beads,
Scouring the lazy spurtle, doughtily,
   They often wipe their reeking, sweating heads;
To crown the scene, the scanty bawbees jingles;
   Each joins a penny, and maun ha'e a smack
Of barley bree, by Robin's cheery ingle,
   To chase 'cauld care awa'', and welcome back
   Sweet blinks of auld langsyne, and gar him laugh and crack.

O, why does stern oppression crush the poor,
   And moral knowledge elevate their hearts?
Doom'd from a master labour to implore,
   And thank him for the mis'ry he imparts.
Ye petty tyrants, puff'd with puny pride,
   Why are your slaves at home in want and gloom?
Why do the poor in poverty abide?
   Philanthropy bewails your hopeless doom,
   Proud intellectual men, slaves of the wretched loom.

ANONYMOUS, 1838

sappy – plump; *gab* – mouth; *fash* – bother; *lowe* – fire
spurtle – stirring stick; *barley bree – whisky; ingle* – fireside; *gar* – make

Cuddle Doon

The bairnies cuddle doon at nicht
   Wi' muckle faucht an' din –
'O, try and sleep, ye waukrife rogues,
   Your faither's comin' in' –
They never heed a word I speak;
   I try to gi'e a froon,
But aye I hap them up, an' cry,
   'O, bairnies, cuddle doon.'

Wee Jamie wi' the curly heid –
   He aye sleeps next the wa' –
Bangs up an' cries, 'I want a piece' –
   The rascal starts them a'.
I rin an' fetch them pieces, drinks,
   They stop awee the soun',
Then draw the blankets up an' cry,
   'Noo, weanies, cuddle doon.'

But ere five minutes gang, wee Rab
   Cries oot, frae 'neath the claes,
'Mither, mak' Tam gi'e ower at ance,
   He's kittling wi' his taes.'
The mischief's in that Tam for tricks,
   He'd bother half the toon;
But aye I hap them up, and cry,
   'O, bairnies, cuddle doon.'

At length they hear their faither's fit,
    An', as he steeks the door,
They turn their faces to the wa',
    While Tam pretends to snore.
'Hae a' the weans been gude?' he asks,
    As he pits aff his shoon.
'The bairnies, John, are in their beds,
    An' lang since cuddled doon.'

An' just afore we bed oorsel's,
    We look at oor wee lambs;
Tam has his airm roun' wee Rab's neck,
    An' Rab his airm roun' Tam's.
I lift wee Jamie up the bed,
    An', as I straik each croon,
I whisper, till my heart fills up,
    'O bairnies, cuddle doon.'

The bairnies cuddle doon at nicht
    Wi' mirth that's dear to me;
But sune the big warl's cark an' care
    Will quaten doon their glee.
Yet, come what will to ilka ane,
    May He who rules aboon
Aye whisper, though their pows be bald,
    'O, bairnies, cuddle doon.'

ALEXANDER ANDERSON (1845–1909)

waukrife – sleepless; *piece* – bread and jam; *kittling* – tickling
hap – tuck up; *cark* – weight; *pows* – heads

from **The Cotter's Saturday Night**

Let not Ambition mock their useful toil,
Their homely joys, and destiny obscure;
Nor Grandeur hear, with a disdainful smile,
The short and simple annals of the Poor.

Gray

II   November chill blaws loud wi' angry sugh;
       The short'ning winter-day is near a close;
    The miry beasts retreating frae the pleugh;
       The black'ning trains o' craws to their repose:
    The toil-worn COTTER frae his labor goes,
       This night his weekly moil is at an end,
    Collects his *spades*, his *mattocks* and his *hoes*,
       Hoping the *morn* in ease and rest to spend,
And weary, o'er the muir, his course does hameward bend.

III   At length his lonely *Cot* appears in view,
       Beneath the shelter of an aged tree;
    Th' expectant wee-things, toddlan, stacher thro'
       To meet their *Dad*, wi' flichterin noise and glee.
    His wee-bit ingle, blinkan bonilie,
       His clean hearth-stane, his thrifty *Wifie*'s smile
    The *lisping infant*, prattling on his knee,
       Does a' his weary kiaugh and care beguile,
And makes him quite forget his labor and his toil.

IV   Belyve, the *elder bairns* come drapping in,
   At *Service* out, amang the Farmers roun';
  Some ca' the pleugh, some herd, some tentie rin
   A cannie errand to a neebor toun:
  Their eldest hope, their *Jenny*, woman-grown,
   In youthfu' bloom, Love sparkling in her e'e,
  Comes hame, perhaps to show a braw new gown,
   Or deposite her sair-won penny-fee,
 To help her *Parents* dear, if they in hardship be.

V   With joy unfeign'd, *brothers* and *sisters* meet,
   And each for other's weelfare kindly speirs:
  The social hours, swift-wing'd, unnotic'd, fleet;
   Each tells the uncos that he sees or hears.
  The *Parents partial* eye their hopeful years;
   Anticipation forward points the view;
  The *Mother* wi' her needle and her sheers
   Gars auld claes look amaist as weel's the new;
 The *Father* mixes a', wi' admonition due.

VI   Their Master's and their Mistress's command,
   The *youngkers* a' are warned to obey;
  And mind their labors wi' an eydent hand,
   And ne'er, tho' out o' sight, to jauk or play:
  'And O! be sure to fear the Lord alway!
   'And mind your *duty*, duely, morn and night!
  'Lest in temptation's path ye gang astray,
   'Implore His counsel and assisting might:
 'They never sought in vain, that sought the Lord aright.'

VII   But hark! a rap comes gently to the door;
              Jenny, wha kens the meaning o' the same,
          Tells how a neebor lad came o'er the muir,
              To do some errands, and convoy her hame.
          The wily Mother sees the *conscious flame*
              Sparkle in *Jenny's* e'e, and flush her cheek,
          With heart-struck, anxious care enquires his name,
              While *Jenny* hafflins is afraid to speak;
          Weel-pleas'd the Mother hears, it's nae wild, worthless *Rake*.

XI   But now the Supper crowns their simple board,
              The healsome *Porritch*, chief of SCOTIA's food:
          The soupe their *only Hawkie* does afford,
              That 'yont the hallan snugly chows her cood:
          The *Dame* brings forth, in complimental mood,
              To grace the lad, her weel-hain'd kebbuck, fell;
          And aft he's prest, and aft he ca's it guid;
              The frugal *Wifie*, garrulous, will tell,
          How 'twas a towmond auld, sin' Lint was i' the bell.

XII   The chearfu' Supper done, wi' serious face,
              They, round the ingle, form a circle wide;
          The Sire turns o'er, with patriarchal grace,
              The big *ha'-Bible*, ance his *Father's* pride:
          His bonnet rev'rently is laid aside,
              His *lyart haffets* wearing thin and bare;
          Those strains that once did sweet in ZION glide,
              He wales a portion with judicious care;
          '*And let us worship GOD!*' he says with solemn air.

XIV   The priest-like Father reads the sacred page,
        How *Abram* was the Friend of GOD on high;
      Or, *Moses* bade eternal warfare wage,
        With *Amalek's* ungracious progeny;
      Or how the *royal Bard* did groaning lye,
        Beneath the stroke of Heaven's avenging ire;
      Or *Job's* pathetic plaint, and wailing cry;
        Or rapt *Isiah's* wild, seraphic fire;
    Or other *Holy Seers* that tune the *sacred lyre*.

XVIII   Then homeward all take off their sev'ral way;
        The youngling *Cottagers* retire to rest:
      The Parent-pair their *secret homage* pay,
        And proffer up to Heaven the warm request,
      That 'HE who stills the *raven's* clam'rous nest,
        'And decks the *lily* fair in flow'ry pride,
      'Would, in the way His *Wisdom* sees the best,
        'For *them* and for their *little ones* provide;
    'But chiefly, in their hearts with *Grace divine* preside.'

XIX   From Scenes like these, old SCOTIA's grandeur springs,
        That makes her lov'd at home, rever'd abroad:
      Princes and lords are but the breath of kings,
        'An honest man's the noble work of GOD:'
      And *certes*, in fair Virtue's heavenly road,
        The *Cottage* leaves the *Palace* far behind:
      What is a lordling's pomp? a cumbrous load,
        Disguising oft the *wretch* of human kind,
    Studied in the arts of Hell, in wickedness refin'd!

XX   O SCOTIA! my dear, my native soil!
           For whom my warmest wish to Heaven is sent!
       Long may thy hardy sons of *rustic toil*
           Be blest with health and peace and sweet content!
       And O may Heaven their simple lives prevent
           From *Luxury's* contagion, weak and vile!
       Then howe'er crowns and *coronets* be rent,
           A *virtuous Populace* may rise the while,
       And stand a wall of fire, around their much-love'd ISLE.

XXI   O THOU! who pour'd the *patriotic tide*,
           That stream'd thro' great, unhappy WALLACE' heart;
       Who dar'd to, nobly, stem tyrannic pride,
           Or *nobly die*, the second glorious part:
       (The Patriot's GOD, peculiarly thou art,
           His *friend*, *inspirer*, *guardian* and *reward*!)
       O never, never SCOTIA's realm desert,
           But still the Patriot, and the Patriot-bard,
       In bright succession raise, her *Ornament* and *Guard*!

ROBERT BURNS (1759–1796)

    sugh – sough; *flichterin* – fluttering; *ingle* – hearth fire
    kiaugh – anxiety; *Belyve* – soon; *tentie* – heedful; *cannie* – careful;
    speirs – asks; *uncos* – news; *eydent* – diligent; *jauk* – idle
    Hawkie – cow; *hallan* – partition
    weel-hain'd kebbuck – hoarded cheese; *towmond* – twelvemonth
    lyart haffets – grizzled locks; *wales* – chooses

Family Visit

Laying linoleum, my father spends hours
with his tape-measure
littering the floor
as he checks his figures, gets
the angle right; then cuts
carefully, to the music
of a slow logic. In despair
I conjure up a room where
a boy sits and plays with coloured bricks.

My mind tugging at its traces,
I see him in more dapper days
outside the Kibble Palace
with my grandfather, having
his snapshot taken; men firing
that year's leaves.
The Gardens are only a stone's throw
from where I live . . . But now
a younger self comes clutching at my sleeve.

Or off to Inellan, singing, we would go,
boarding the steamer at the Broomielaw
in broad summer, these boomps-a-daisy
days, the ship's band playing in a lazy
swell, my father steering well clear
of the bar, mother making neat
packets of waste-paper to carry

to the nearest basket or (more likely)
all the way back to Cranworth Street.

Leaving my father at it
(he'd rather be alone) I take
my mother through the changed Botanics.
The bandstand is gone, and the great
rain-barrels that used to rot
and overflow. Everything is neat
and plastic. And it is I who must walk
slowly for her, past the sludge
and pocked granite of Queen Margaret Bridge.

STEWART CONN (b.1936)

The Farmer's Ingle

Et multo in primis hilarans convivia Baccho,
Ante focum, si frigus erit.

Virgil. Buc.

Whan gloming grey out o'er the welkin keeks,
    Whan Batie ca's his owsen to the byre,
Whan Thrasher John, sair dung, his barn-door steeks,
    And lusty lasses at the dighting tire:
What bangs fu' leal the e'enings coming cauld,
    And gars snaw-tapit winter freeze in vain;
Gars dowie mortals look baith blyth and bauld,
    Nor fley'd wi' a' the poortith o' the plain;
      Begin my Muse, and chant in hamely strain.

Frae the big stack, weel winnow't on the hill,
    Wi' divets theekit frae the weet and drift,
Sods, peats, and heath'ry trufs the chimley fill,
    And gar their thick'ning smeek salute the lift;
The gudeman, new come hame, is blyth to find,
    Whan he out o'er the halland flings his een,
That ilka turn is handled to his mind,
    That a' his housie looks sae cosh and clean,
      For cleanly house looes he, tho' e'er sae mean.

Weel kens the gudewife that the pleughs require
    A heartsome meltith, and refreshing synd
O' nappy liquor, o'er a bleezing fire:
    Sair wark and poortith douna weel be join'd.

Wi' butter'd bannocks now the girdle reeks,
    I' the far nook the bowie briskly reams;
The readied kail stand by the chimley cheeks,
    And had the riggin het wi' welcome steams,
    Whilk than the daintiest kitchen nicer seems.

Frae this lat gentler gabs a lesson lear;
    Wad they to labouring lend an eidant hand,
They'd rax fell strang upo' the simplest fare,
    Nor find their stamacks ever at a stand.
Fu' hale and healthy wad they pass the day,
    At night in calmest slumbers dose fu' sound,
Nor doctor need their weary life to spae,
    Nor drogs their noddle and their sense confound,
    Till death slip sleely on, and gi'e the hindmost wound.

On sicken food has mony a doughty deed
    By Caledonia's ancestors been done;
By this did mony wight fu' weirlike bleed
    In brulzies frae the dawn to set o' sun:
'Twas this that brac'd their gardies, stiff and strang,
    That bent the deidly yew in antient days,
Laid Denmark's daring sons on yird alang,
    Gar'd Scottish thristles bang the Roman bays;
    For near our crest their heads they doughtna raise.

The couthy cracks begin whan supper's o'er,
    The cheering bicker gars them glibly gash
O' simmer's showery blinks and winters sour,
    Whase floods did erst their mailins produce hash:
'Bout kirk and market eke their tales gae on,

How Jock woo'd Jenny here to be his bride,
And there how Marion, for a bastard son,
    Upo' the cutty-stool was forced to ride,
    The waefu' scald o' our Mess John to bide.

The fient a chiep's amang the bairnies now;
    For a' their anger's wi' their hunger gane:
Ay maun the childer, wi' a fastin mou',
    Grumble and greet, and make an unco mane,
In rangles round before the ingle's low:
    Frae gudame's mouth auld warld tale they hear,
O' warlocks louping round the wirrikow,
    O' gaists that win in glen and kirk-yards drear,
    Whilk touzles a' their tap, and gars them shak wi' fear.

For weel she trows that fiends and fairies be
    Sent frae the de'il to fleetch us to our ill;
That ky hae tint their milk wi' evil eie,
    And corn been scowder'd on the glowing kill.
O mock na this, my friends! but rather mourn,
    Ye in life's brawest spring wi' reason clear,
Wi' eild our idle fancies a' return,
    And dim our dolefu' days wi' bairnly fear;
    The mind's ay cradled whan the grave is near.

Yet thrift, industrious, bides her latest days,
    Tho' age her sair dow'd front wi' runcles wave,
Yet frae the russet lap the spindle plays,
    Her e'enin stent reels she as weel's the lave.
On some feast-day, the wee-things buskit braw
    Shall heeze her heart up wi' a silent joy,

Fu' cadgie that her head was up and saw
    Her ain spun cleething on a darling oy,
    Careless tho' death shou'd make the feast her foy.

In its auld lerroch yet the deas remains,
    Where the gudeman aft streeks him at his ease,
A warm and canny lean for weary banes
    O' lab'rers doil'd upo' the wintry leas:
Round him will badrins and the colly come,
    To wag their tail, and cast a thankfu' eie
To him wha kindly flings them mony a crum
    O' kebbuck whang'd, and dainty fadge to prie;
    This a' the boon they crave, and a' the fee.

Frae him the lads their morning counsel tak,
    What stacks he wants to thrash, what rigs to till;
How big a birn maun lie on bassie's back,
    For meal and multure to the thirling mill.
Niest the gudewife her hireling damsels bids
    Glowr thro' the byre, and see the hawkies bound,
Take tent case Crummy tak her wonted tids,
    And ca' the leglin's treasure on the ground,
    Whilk spills a kebbuck nice, or yellow pound.

Then a' the house for sleep begin to grien,
    Their joints to slack frae industry a while;
The leaden god fa's heavy on their ein,
    And hafflins steeks them frae their daily toil;
The cruizy too can only blink and bleer,
    The restit ingle's done the maist it dow;
Tacksman and cottar eke to bed maun steer,

Upo' the cod to clear their drumly pow,
Till wauken'd by the dawning's ruddy glow.

Peace to the husbandman and a' his tribe,
    Whase care fells a' our wants frae year to year;
Lang may his sock and couter turn the gleyb,
    And bauks o' corn bend down wi' laded ear.
May Scotia's simmers ay look gay and green,
    Her yellow har'sts frae scowry blasts decreed;
May a' her tenants sit fu' snug and bien,
    Frae the hard grip of ails and poortith freed,
    And a lang lasting train o' peaceful hours succeed.

ROBERT FERGUSSON (1750–74)

gloming – gloaming, dusk; *owsen* – oxen; *dung* – driven; *steeks* – shuts;
dighting – winnowing grain; *bangs* – crams; *leal* – truly; *gars* – makes;
dowie – gloomy; *poortith* – poverty; *divets* – turfs; *theekit* – thatched;
drift – snow; *halland* – partition; *cosh* – comfortable; *meltith* – meal;
synd – draught; *nappy* – ale; *bowie* – small barrel; *reams* – creams; *kail* – broth;
riggin – top of house; *gabs* – gossips; *lear* – learn; *rax* – grow; *brulzies* – fights;
gardies – arms; *yird* – earth; *gash* – chat; *mailins* – farms; *hash* – damage;
cutty stool – stool of repentance; *fient* – devil; *chiep* – chirruping, whispering;
mane – whinge; *rangles* – clusters; *wirrikow* – devil, devil's imp; *fleetch* – coax;
tint – lost; *scowder'd* – scorched; *kill* – kiln; *dow'd* – withered; *lave* – rest;
buskit – ready dressed; *heeze* – lift; *cadgie* – happy; *oy* – grandchild;
foy – farewell meal; *lerroch* – appointed place; *deas* – seat; *streeks* – stretches;
doil'd – exhausted; *badrins* – cat; *kebbuck whang'd* – cheese sliced;
fadge – bannock; *prie* – taste; *birn* – burden; *bassie* – old horse;
thirling – grinding; *hawkies* – cows; *tids* – temper fits; *ca'* – overturn;
leglin – milking pail; *grien* – long for; *hafflins* – partly; *steeks* – shuts;
cruizy – oil lamp; *restit* – burned out; *dow* – can; *tacksman and cottar* – farm
tenants; *cod* – pillow; *drumly* – troubled; *pow* – head; *sock* – ploughshare;
couter – cutter in front of the ploughshare; *bauks* – strips of land; *scowry* –
showery; *bien* – prosperous

Lernin

thi wummin iz standin
by thi doar
thi wee boy iz rite
inside thi shoap
thi man iz bitween
thi wummin
an thi boy

thi wee boy iz greetin
wi hiz hole body
thi wee shoodurz
shuddur
inside thi bobbly lookn
jumpur wi
sumthin sticky smujd
doon thi frunt
teerz make white scarz
throo thi muck
oan hiz crumply face

thi man goze
fukn MOOV
ah telt yi
moov it
NOW

the wee laddy
greets hardur
mummy
he sayz
hiz arms reechin up
tay hur
mummy ah wont YOO
mummy PLEEZ

thi wummin
looks it thi boy
hur eyebrows rinkul
hur body twitchiz
taywordz thi bairn
then she stops
looks it thi man

jist yoo stay
rite thare hen
he sayz
ahv telt ye bifore
dinny giv inty him
thi boyz goaty lern
yi heer mi?
thi boyz goaty lern

ALISON FLETT (b.1965)

The Drunkard's Wife

O Jeanie, my woman! whar is't ye are gaun,
Wi' a bairn on yer arm an' ane in yer haun?
There's snaw on the grun, an' nae shoon on yer feet,
And ye speak na a word, but jist murther an' greet.

Yer ae drogget coat is baith scrimpy an' worn,
An' yer aul leloc toush is baith dirty an' torn;
An' roun' yer lean haffits, ance sonsy and fair,
Hings tautit an' tousie yer bonny broun hair.

Yer wee shilpit weanie's a pityfu' prufe
That yer bosom's as dry an' as queem as my lufe;
For the bairn wi' the beard sooks ye sairest alace,
For he draws the red bluid frae yer hert an' yer face.

Waesucks for ye, Jeanie! I kent ye fu' weel
When a lass; ye war couthie, an' cantie, an' leal:
Wi' cheeks like the roses, yer bonnie blue ee,
Aye glancin' an' dancin' wi' daffin an' glee.

They tauld ye that Davie was keen o' the drink,
That siller ne'er baid in his pouches a blink;
An' a' he got claut o' he waret on the dram,
An' ae pay ne'er sert till anither ane cam.

But ye wadna be warnt, sae yer wierd ye maun dree,
Tho' aften ye raither wad lie doun an' dee;
For o' puir drucken Davie ye've nae houp ava,
Sae yer greetin', an' toilin', an' fechtin' awa.

JANET HAMILTON (1795–1873)

murther – whimper; *greet* – cry; *drogget* – coarse woolen cloth;
leloc – lilac; *toush* – jacket or dress; *haffits* – cheeks;
tautit – matted; *tousie* – dishevelled; *shilpit* – shrunken, puny;
queem – flat, smooth; *lufe* – palm of hand; *alace* – alas;
couthie – friendly; *cantie* – cheerful; *leal* – true; *claut* – hold;
waret – spent; *wierd* – fate; *dree* – endure

The Harvest in March

The drive from Elgin to the hospital
had no tree felled across the way, no snow,
instead the March light opened our road east,
back from the blue beyond of Bennachie.
It cast itself across the stubbled parks,
and hours of sun seemed left in Aberdeen,
and so we walked out for the last time as
a couple. In the chipper you announced
'It's coming,' and you squatted, scaring both
me and the granite wifies serving me.

Twelve hours gave you your own geography:
a canal with a head stuck in it, so
they reached for forcing drugs, the opening knife,
and that domestic-looking suction plug
which pulled a girl out like a plum, still on
her stalk, since in the country inside you
it's always autumn. Wheeched her wheezing off
to thread her little nostrils with those tubes
that syphon out the faeces. Which looked like
she was being stitched onto our loud world.

And when I brought her back they'd stitched you too:
you chatted with the surgeon as he finished
your perineum like a trout fly, and
I handed you our daughter in a towel.

W. N. HERBERT (b.1961)

Crystal Set

Just as the stars appear, father
carries from his garden shed
a crystal set, built
as per instructions
in the *Amateur Mechanic*.
Mother dries her hands. Their boy
and ginger cat lie beside the fire.
He's reading – what – *Treasure Island* –
but jumps to clear the dresser. Hush,
they tell each other. Hush!

The silly baby bangs her spoon
as they lean in to radio-waves
which lap, the boy imagines,
just like Scarborough. Indeed,
it *is* the sea they hear as though
the brown box were a shell. Dad
sorts through fizz, until, like diamonds
lost in the dust – '*Listen, Ships' Morse!*' –
and the boy grips his chair. As though
he'd risen sudden as an angel
to gaze down, he understands
that not his house, not
Scarborough Beach, but the whole
Island of Britain
is washed by dark waves. Hush
they tell each other. Hush.

There is nothing to tune to
but Greenwich pips
and the anxious signalling
of ships that nudge our shores.
Dumb silent waves. But that
was then. Now, gentle listener,
it's time to take our leave
of Mum and Dad's proud glow, the boy's
uncertain smile. Besides,
the baby's asleep.
So let's tune out here
and slip along the dial. *Hush.*

KATHLEEN JAMIE (b.1962)

from The Big Sister Poems

The Message

Little brother I got a message for you
not from Santa no
it's from Da.
Listen will you.

See before you got born
see Da still had a job to do.
We got bacon and eggs for breakfast.
Ma used to afford to get a hair-do.

Then she goes and gets pregnant again
and even although it was by accident
Da said we could maybe still afford it.
He meant you.

It turns out we can't.

The other thing is
this room before you came along
only had the one bed in it.
Mine.

See there isn't really room for the two.
So what with one thing and another
and since you were the last to arrive
Da says you've to go little brother.

Here is your bag it's packed ready
with your beanos pyjamas and a few
biscuits for when you get hungry
I'm sure you'll be better off wherever

you end up so good luck and
goodbye.

A Bedtime Story

There was a bottle with a dream in it.
Da drank from it because
this dream made everything seem
a lot better than they was.

A boring word sounded cleverer
and like it might mean more
and even his jokes sounded funnier
than they ever been before.

The dream it made Da swagger
and laugh and drink up more
till swagger turned into stagger
and laugh turned into roar.

Then the dream turned into a bad dream
and it made Da curse and swore.
So when he got back home at last
well he banged the front door.

See Da in this dream is someone

who knows when he's always right
so when Ma went and argued with him
they started to shout and fight.

They fight about Da and his dreaming
see then the nightmare goes on
he's hitting her now she's screaming
then this morning Ma's gone.

And Da says he can't remember
what the dream was all about.
So he goes out to look for her.
Don't ask me how I found this out.

I'm yer big sister amn't I.
I know things you don't that's all.
Like the story of the bottle with a dream in it
a dream called that's right

now get to sleep.

The Lesson

I'll tell you what now little brother
I'm going to teach you something
you'll never ever forget.

You go half way upstairs that's right.
You turn round you shut your eyes.
You keep them shut tight.

Now on the count of five
now I want you to jump.
Now is that clear.

Don't be scared little brother.
I'll be standing at the bottom here
to catch you so be brave.

1 . . . 2 . . . 3 . . . 4 . . .

Five I said I'd teach you something
this is it don't trust anybody.
When you're older you'll thank me for it.

Shut up.

BRIAN McCABE (b.1951)

The World Book of the McMillans

Dear **Hugh McMillan**,
you have been selected by our clan computer
to receive a copy of
The World Book of the McMillans $149.95
(including unique hand painted coat of arms).
Have you ever considered, Hugh McMillan,
your family ties and heritage?
In these pages, **Hugh**,
you will bear witness to the heroism
and industriousness of your ancestors
and learn about the forebears
who shaped the history of the world,
like **Fergus McMillan, the 8th Man of Moidart**,
Hector 'Steamboats' McMillan,
the inventor of the 12 Bore Scrotal Pump Beam,
Brian 'Big Shuggie' McMillan, Golf Caddie to the Stars,
and many many others,
though probably not **Archie McMillan**
who died of silicosis
or **James and Colin** who drowned in the Minch,
or **Struan** who drank himself to death
in that corner of the Central Bar.
To bear witness to that kind of thing,
Hugh McMillan,
it costs a bit more.

HUGH McMILLAN (b.1955)

Childhood

Long time he lay upon the sunny hill,
    To his father's house below securely bound.
Far off the silent, changing sound was still,
    With the black islands lying thick around.

He saw each separate height, each vaguer hue,
    Where the massed islands rolled in mist away,
And though all ran together in his view
    He knew that unseen straits between them lay.

Often he wondered what new shores were there.
    In thought he saw the still light on the sand,
The shallow water clear in tranquil air,
    And walked through it in joy from strand to strand.

Over the sound a ship so slow would pass
    That in the black hill's gloom it seemed to lie.
The evening sound was smooth like sunken glass,
    And time seemed finished ere the ship passed by.

Grey tiny rocks slept round him where he lay,
    Moveless as they, more still as evening came,
The grasses threw straight shadows far away,
    And from the house his mother called his name.

EDWIN MUIR (1887–1959)

Sleepless

In *medianoche*, they find themselves –
a father and his two children,
unable to sleep through the ever-
gathering heat of themselves –
sitting in their pants
round the kitchen table, a plastic flagon
of fridge-cold water emptying
before their eyes. There is something
secretive meeting like this –
the children's naked chests
brushing the table's edge, as upstairs
their mother sleeps on,
wound in her tangle of sheets.
Though, whatever the secret is,
it remains unspoken, shared
like a scent of hilltop thyme.
If, that is, a scent could be seen
through a film of sleep –
in the way, just say, the boy had earlier
watched his sister from below the surface
of the pool, as she wind-milled
into water, hair flaring
above her, the water giving her
the graceful movements
of the dancer she is. Moments later,
he had popped up, raising goggles, wiping eyes.
How did I look? she'd asked. *How did I look?*

They sit composed now, slightly slumped,
sculpted by the kitchen light, as the moon
gives shape to the olive trees, the stones
in the fields, the fallen almonds. They are a family,
once all activity has been stripped from them.
And they sit, mostly in silence, sifting through
this air, this love, the faintest scent of thyme.

TOM POW (b.1949)

The Land of Story-Books

At evening, when the lamp is lit,
Around the fire my parents sit;
They sit at home and talk and sing,
And do not play at anything.

Now, with my little gun, I crawl
All in the dark along the wall,
And follow round the forest track
Away behind the sofa back.

There, in the night, where none can spy,
All in my hunter's camp I lie,
And play at books that I have read
Till it is time to go to bed.

These are the hills, these are the woods,
These are my starry solitudes;
And there the river by whose brink
The roaring lions come to drink.

I see the others far away
As if in firelit camp they lay,
And I, like to an Indian scout,
Around their party prowled about.

So, when my nurse comes in for me,
Home I return across the sea,
And go to bed with backward looks
At my dear land of Story-books.

ROBERT LOUIS STEVENSON (1850–94)

Festive Family Photo

Father sprouting Christmas tree
            from his bald patch

Son surprised between pulled faces
            saying cheese

Daughter between sugar and spice
            showing teeth

Mother escaping the picture
            by taking it

HAMISH WHYTE (b.1947)

Grandmother

carries the guid Scots tongue in her heid
all the way to London

where it becomes like the kitchen china
worn and cracked with use

kept in the press with the girdle and the spurtle,
the ashet and the jeelie pan.

The good china of English
is what you bring out for visitors:

kept in the credenza
with the key in its lock.

Lift it carefully onto the silver-plated tray.
Remember which language

you're speaking in. Dinnae –
Dinnae forget.

ELIZABETH BURNS (b.1957)

My Grandfather

His head was grand and mottled as a planet.
There were no maps: his rage sprang up
mysterious as geysers. The continents
were dark where his several brothers
lived (though Uncle James from Africa
once showed up in the flesh) and if
there were, in the frozen poles, the hole
he'd put his father in, long ago, I never knew
nor dared to ask. He was munificent
and vast. This is all I know for sure:

Grandad looked like old Duke Wayne
and shot birds with the Earl of Cairn.
He had cigars and a Jaguar, and his father
was a gas fitter. He beat us all at dominoes,
but drew black/black one day and died.
Because of him we're not self-made.
He left us that, Aunt Katie's rug
and a drawer full of cashmere socks,
luxurious and muffling, easily worn to holes.

KATE CLANCHY (b.1965)

Photograph of my Grandparents

(A Wartime Romance)

England.   An oval of leafy sepia scribble
an ideogram of rural idyll   even in Weybridge
even in wartime

Keith Macfarlane, a New Zealand soldier   Connie Renton
a girl in uniform, have paused   bicycles askew
against that sunlit aura

The photograph is a charmed circle
beyond it lie the churned and broken fields of Flanders
Gallipoli's reef of ANZAC bone

It is she, the ambulance driver   who has transported him
(After the desert war, light without mercy   he feels
TB's scorching fire a kind of balm)

Is he serious or quizzical under his brimmed hat?
In fact, he would like to crack a joke   Poms
are so solemn   part of his convalescence is a mission
to upset the occasion   to make them laugh

Connie smiles
seeing him   she imagines a country without loss
a way of mending the families broken by death

They are drawn into love's charmed circle   their pain
lies beyond it, fading   like the sepia's rosy margin

This is a wartime romance   he is
her handsome soldier   she is his Scottish lass

GERRIE FELLOWS (b.1954)

Grandma as a Genie

It happened in the middle of the school play.
I was a Chinese genie. 'Command
thy humble servant to appear,' I said.
And did. It was then that Grandma vanished.

I'd given her the idea. I believe she jumped
into the urn she kept on the window sill
and which was so tall she could stand upright
inside it without in the least disturbing
the knife-sharp pleats of the skirt she wore.

Grandma liked things tidy. And provided
she kept her shoulders taut and her arms
in, she'd have fitted the urn very nicely.
I knew she was in there. Sharp-pleated
and furious. Nobody's humble servant.

DIANA HENDRY (b.1941)

Grandpa's Soup

No one makes soup like my Grandpa's,
with its diced carrots the perfect size
and its diced potatoes the perfect size
and its wee soft bits –
what are their names?
and its big bit of hough,
which rhymes with loch, floating
like a rich island in the middle of the soup sea.

I say, Grandpa, Grandpa your soup is the best
     soup in the whole world.
And Grandpa says, Och,
which rhymes with hough and loch,
Och, don't be daft,
because he's shy about his soup, my Grandpa.
He knows I will grow up and pine for it.
I will fall ill and desperately need it.
I will long for it my whole life after he is gone.
Every soup will become sad and wrong after he is gone.
He knows when I'm older I will avoid soup altogether.
Oh Grandpa, Grandpa, why is your soup so glorious? I say
tucking into my fourth bowl in a day.

Barley! That's the name of the wee soft bits.
Barley.

JACKIE KAY (b.1961)

hough – hock, hind-leg joint of meat

For My Grandmother Knitting

There is no need they say
but the needles still move
their rhythms in the working of your hands
as easily
as if your hands
were once again those sure and skilful hands
of the fisher-girl.

You are old now
and your grasp of things is not so good
but master of your moments then
deft and swift
you slit the still-ticking quick silver fish.
Hard work it was too
of necessity.

But now they say there is no need
as the needles move
in the working of your hands
once the hands of the bride
with the hand-span waist
once the hands of the miner's wife
who scrubbed his back
in a tin bath by the coal fire
once the hands of the mother
of six who made do and mended
scraped and slaved slapped sometimes
when necessary.

But now they say there is no need
the kids they say grandma
have too much already
more than they can wear
too many scarves and cardigans –
gran you do too much
there's no necessity.

At your window you wave
them goodbye Sunday.
With your painful hands
big on shrunken wrists.
Swollen-jointed. Red. Arthritic. Old.
But the needles still move
their rhythms in the working of your hands
easily
as if your hands remembered
of their own accord the pattern
as if your hands had forgotten
how to stop.

LIZ LOCHHEAD (b.1947)

Grandchild

She stumbles upon every day
as though it were a four-leaf clover
ringed in a horseshoe.

The light is her luck – and its thickening
into chair, postman, poodle
with a ribbon round its neck.

She plays among godsends
and becomes one. Watch her being
a seal or a sleepy book.

Yet sometimes she wakes in the night
terrified, staring
at somewhere else.

She's learning that ancestors
refuse to be dead. Their resurrection
is her terror.

We soothe the little godsend
back to us
and pray, despairingly –

May the clover be
a true prophet. May her light be
without history.

NORMAN MacCAIG (1910–96)

from **Stone**

My grandfather, when he was old,
would sit for hours above the village,
poised on the hillside like a rock.
If you crept up behind him you could hear
him muttering, a curse and a curse and a curse.
He dredged the decades and there was no one
from the carpenter who made his cradle onwards
he didn't curl his tongue around,
no incident since his incidents began
he couldn't remould nearer to his heart's desire.
It was an education to sit and listen –
the time someone did this ... did that ...
the time ... the time ... the time –
over and over again, obsessively, adoringly,
he told his wounds. Longevity in the making.
His soft coevals fell away, destroyed by love,
and from their funerals he walked home clinking.
Seventy, eighty, ninety upwards.
He was still muttering when he took to bed
and there was never the least crack in him.

ALASDAIR MACLEAN (1926–94)

Grandchild

Before he's born you can't understand
what the fuss is about. You're not
even bothered about having one.

Friends bore you with incessant chat
about their sleeping patterns, eating patterns,
bowel movements, the funny things they say.

They always have packs of photos
taken from every angle, and you
wonder if they know there's a war on.

And then your own love affair begins.
He is exceptionally beautiful of course
everyone will want to see the photographs,

will want to listen when you tell them
all the funny things he does, how well he sleeps
how very, very special he is.

And your dear grandmother friends
who know all about this obsessive love
indulge you, agree he is exceptionally beautiful.

And you discover that their incessant chat
about their grandchildren is compelling
and the war can wait.

PAULINE PRIOR-PITT (b.1940)

Five Years Later

I kneel down in the room my mother's died in,
not to pray, not to weep:
I touch her hand again and say her name aloud.

*

Five years later I'm catching up on Sarajevo,
current famines, weapon stockpiles (outside
the city's wounds are opening again:

hospitals and schools stand gutted;
addicts sweat, get sick; the mad
and destitute seek us out)

when all at once the paper I've been reading,
the kitchen I am sitting in, our tenement, our street
and Edinburgh itself seem set around me
as the walls of her room.

Too late to kneel down, too late to pray
to weep, to take her hand –

The loss I'm grieving for is still to come:

Sometimes I see it in another's eyes.
Sometimes I see it in my own.

RON BUTLIN (b.1949)

Opera

Throw all your stagey chandeliers in wheelbarrows and
    move them north
To celebrate my mother's sewing-machine
And her beneath an eighty-watt bulb, pedalling
Iambs on an antique metal footplate
Powering the needle through its regular lines,
Doing her work. To me as a young boy
That was her typewriter. I'd watch
Her hands and feet in unison, or read
Between her calves the wrought-iron letters:
SINGER. Mass-produced polished wood and metal,
It was a powerful instrument. I stared
Hard at its brilliant needle's eye that purred
And shone at night; and then each morning after
I went to work at school, wearing her songs.

ROBERT CRAWFORD (b.1959)

Dressing Mother

I help roll her stockings over her feet,
then up to her knees. She's managed her dress
but I free her fingers from the sleeves.
Before the mirror she rouges her cheeks,
combs her thin curls, hands me a bow.
It's scarlet and goes on a ribbon I thread
under her collar and fix with a hook.
Over an hour to dress her today.

Such an innocence stays at the nape of the neck
it fumbles my fingers. I see her binding
bands of scarlet at the ends of my plaits
and fastening the buttons at my back.
Now look – she's dressed as a child off
to some party. I straighten her scarlet bow.

and don't want her to go,
don't want her to go.

DIANA HENDRY (b.1941)

from **The Adoption Papers,**
Chapter 6: The Telling Part

Ma mammy bot me oot a shop
Ma mammy says I was a luvly baby

Ma Mammy picked me (I wiz the best)
your mammy had to take you (she'd no choice)

Ma Mammy says she's no really ma mammy
(just kid on)

*

But I love ma mammy whether she's real or no

*

She took me when I'd nowhere to go
my mammy is the best mammy in the world OK.

After mammy telt me she wisnae my real mammy
I was scared to death she was gonnie melt
or something or mibbe disappear in the dead
of night and somebody would say she wis a fairy
godmother. So the next morning I felt her skin
to check it was flesh, but mibbe it was just
a good imitation. How could I tell if my mammy
was a dummy with a voice spoken by someone else?
So I searches the whole house for clues
but I never found nothing. Anyhow a day after
I got my guinea pig and forgot all about it.

JACKIE KAY (b.1961)

I Kin See Richt Thru My Mither

My mother always said you could see right through me,
and on winter days she was the first to notice
if I was peally wally, when I looked like her father's
peeweet, his miner's singlet, the colour of lapwing's wings.

My voice plummeting or flying too high was picked up,
if I was peesie-weesie or perskeet, she'd remember
the names of the girls in her class and recite them
like a lovely kirk service, how those eight tight friends

played peever, and how my mother's hair back then
travelled the length of her back, thick-thick
until it had to be shaved off, Oh god, bloody awful.
On days when my wings were grey and still,

my mother's stories of herself as a girl flew around
our house like Uncle Wullie's, from Lochgelly, birds
in his home-made aviary, such pretty colours, chests puffed
as Aunt Ag's puff pastry, my mother brought the colour back,

to my winter face. Stories of mine shafts and pewter tubs,
the long lengths of miners' backs washed for a penny;
the days when the past was so dreamy it seemed it was lived
by somebody else; the days we savoured her past like ghosts.

JACKIE KAY (b.1961)

peally wally – sickly-looking; *peeweet* – lapwing / blue-grey miner's singlet;
peesie-weesie – whining, complaining; *perskeet* – difficult to please;
peever – hopscotch

Sorting Through

The moment she died, my mother's dance dresses
turned from the colours they really were
to the colours I imagine them to be.
I can feel the weight of bumptoed silver shoes
swinging from their anklestraps as she swaggers
up the path towards *her* dad, light-headed
from airman's kisses. Here, at what I'll have to learn
to call *my father's house*, yes every
ragbag scrap of duster prints her even more vivid
than an Ilford snapshot on some seafront
in a white cardigan and that exact frock.
Old lipsticks. Liquid stockings.
Labels like *Harella*, *Gor-ray*, *Berketex*.
As I manhandle whole outfits into binbags for Oxfam
every mote in my eye is a utility mark
and this is useful:
the sadness of dispossessed dresses,
the decency of good coats roundshouldered
in the darkness of wardrobes,
the gravitas of lapels,
the invisible danders of skin fizzing off from them
like all that life that will not neatly end.

LIZ LOCHHEAD (b.1947)

Sang

There's a reid lowe in yer cheek,
Mither, and a licht in yer ee,
And ye sing like the shuilfie in the slae,
But no' for me.

The man that cam' the day,
Mither, that ye ran to meet,
He drapt his gun and fondlet ye
And I was left to greet.

Ye served him kail frae the pat,
Mither, and meat frae the bane.
Ye brocht him cherries frae the gean,
And I gat haurdly ane.

And noo he lies in yer bed,
Mither, and the licht grows dim,
And the sang ye sing as ye hap me ower
Is meant for him.

ROBERT McLELLAN (1907–1985)

lowe – fire; shuilfie – chaffinch; *slae* – sloe; *kail* – broth;
gean – cherry tree; *hap me ower* – tuck me in

Be-Ro

The pages have browned like the gingerbread,
the rock cakes, treacle scones and Victoria sponges
she used to bake for us.

The pancake recipes are almost illegible,
stuck together years ago
by drops of ancient batter.

Not that she would have needed a recipe,
after the dozens she had flipped
on old kitchen ranges, girdles and stoves.

Just above the Madeira Cake
the small hand of one of her daughters
has pencilled in: This BoOk BeLongs to MUMMY.

Next to the Cherry Cake and Melting Moments
her own handwriting runs down the page
multiplying the ingredients by three or four.

I don't remember ever thanking her,
as the still warm baking disappeared
like snow off a dyke.

ANGELA McSEVENEY (b.1964)

Mother, Dear Mother

She is invigilator; her name is knife.
She changes nappies and sleeps in my father's bed.

If I cry blazes or trickle, she'll come to my whistle
And give me her breast. Or let me lie and cry.

Half of her's mine, and half is my hot fat father's.
To each, one arm, one eye – and then what?

What is the good of possessing half a woman?
I'll pull her down to me by her swinging hair

And eat her all up, moon-face, belly and toes,
And throw the skin to my father, to keep him warm.

ELMA MITCHELL (1919–2000)

The Coals

Before my mother's hysterectomy
she cried, and told me she must never bring
coals in from the cellar outside the house,
someone must do it for her. The thing itself
I knew was nothing, it was the thought
of that dependence. Her tears shocked me
like a blow. As once she had been taught,
I was taught self-reliance, discipline,
which is both good and bad. You get things done,
you feel you keep the waste and darkness back
by acts and acts and acts and acts and acts,
bridling if someone tells you this is vain,
learning at last in pain. Hardest of all
is to forgive yourself for things undone,
guilt that can poison life – away with it,
you say, and it is loath to go away.
I learned both love and joy in a hard school
and treasure them like the fierce salvage of
some wreck that has been built to look like stone
and stand, though it did not, a thousand years.

EDWIN MORGAN (b.1920)

Milk

Your custom often
when the house was still

to brew milky coffee
and reminisce.

Child care experts would have frowned
on my late hours,

the bitter adult drinks
and frothy confidences.

Yet your stories stopped my mewling
and continued as I grew

me tending the fire,
you talking of Ireland,

more real to your first born
than the younger ones who slept.

Those nightcaps, Mother,
were our hushed bond.

And though, for twenty years now,
I've drunk my coffee black,

I'm not weaned yet
of that rich, warm milk.

DONNY O'ROURKE (b.1959)

Sonnet – My Mother
(St Leonard's, Edinburgh, 1826)

A pebbled path led up to the door
Where I was born, with holly hedge confined,
Whose leaves the winter snows oft interlined;
Oft now it seems, because the year before
My sister died, we were together more,
And from the parlour window every morn
Looked on that hedge, while mother's face, so worn
With fear of coming ill, bent sweetly o'er.
And when she saw me watching, smile would she,
And turn away with many things distraught;
Thus was it manhood took me by surprise,
The sadness of her heart came into me,
And everything I ever yet have thought
I learned then from her anxious loving eyes.

WILLIAM BELL SCOTT (1811–90)

'You lived in Glasgow'

You lived in Glasgow many years ago.
I do not find your breath in the air.
It was, I think, in the long-skirted thirties
when idle men stood at every corner
chewing their fag-ends of a failed culture.
Now I sit here in George Square
where the War Memorial's yellow sword glows bright
and the white stone lions mouth at bus and car.
A maxi-skirted girl strolls by.
I turn and look. It might be you. But no.
Around me there's a 1970 sky.

Everywhere there are statues. Stone remains.
The mottled flesh is transient. On those trams,
invisible now but to the mind, you bore
your groceries home to the 1930s slums.
'There was such warmth,' you said. The gaslight hums
and large caped shadows tremble on the stair.
Now everything is brighter. Pale ghosts walk
among the spindly chairs, the birchen trees.
In lights of fiercer voltage you are less
visible than when in winter you
walked, a black figure, through the gaslit blue.

The past's an experience that we cannot share.
Flat-capped Glaswegians and the Music Hall.
Apples and oranges on an open stall.
A day in the country. And the sparkling Clyde

splashing its local sewage at the wall.
This April day shakes memories in a shade
opening and shutting like a parasol.
There is no site for the unshifting dead.
You're buried elsewhere though your flickering soul
is a constant tenant of my tenement.

You were happier here than anywhere, you said.
Such fine neighbours helping when your child
almost died of croup. Those pleasant Wildes
removed with the fallen rubble have now gone
in the building programme which renews each stone.
I stand in a cleaner city, better fed,
in my diced coat, brown hat, my paler hands
leafing a copy of the latest book.
Dear ghosts, I love you, haunting sunlit winds,
dear happy dented ghosts, dear prodigal folk.

I left you, Glasgow, at the age of two
and so you are my birthplace just the same.
Divided city of the green and blue
I look for her in you, my constant aim
to find a ghost within a close who speaks
in Highland Gaelic.
                        The bulldozer breaks
raw bricks to powder. Boyish workmen hang
like sailors in tall rigging. Buildings sail
into the future. The old songs you sang
fade in their pop songs, scale on dizzying scale.

IAIN CRICHTON SMITH (1928–98)

Father and the Silver Salver

As was his custom at
approx. 9 a.m. he returned
from the yard for coffee,

would plant his cap on the
silver salver on the hall table
and announce he was home.

He'd been on the go from
6 a.m. to yard, office, harbour.
He brought into the house

salt airs, left on the door-mat
sequins of herring scales
that flashed in the sunlight.

On this fine morning the cap
did not leave the hand.
No salver. He minded

he'd met a couple, man
pushing a two-wheeled
flat-topped float, wife

walking alongside with shut face.
On top a pile of rags, clothing,
mebbe all their worldly goods.

Down Victoria Street he went.

No sighting. The way south,
Saltoun Place, out of town,

he overtook them, paced them,
the while one hand lifting
the rags, slipping from them

the silver salver. No word spoken.
They went their way, he his.

GEORGE BRUCE (1909–2002)

The Field

Afterwards, my father walked to The Mare:
one of the far fields on the hill of Barcraig
crowned by a crescent of elder and chestnut.

He listened to the calls of the curlew and peewit
remembered shafts of light and summer days
recognised the breeze as an endless breath

over rough acres fenced but never fully tamed:
large clumps of whin, thistles, rye grass
a heart of marsh reeds sloping to the burn.

He looked to Muirshiel's dark and brackened hills
round to the hard won grazing of the Law,
and further to the creep of city high rise.

He raised one strong arm across his body
then with the grace of a sower's wide arc
scattered his father to the wind.

JIM CARRUTH (b.1963)

My Faither Sees Me

My faither sees me throu the gless;
why is he out there in the mirk?
His luik gaes throu me like a dirk,
and mine throu his, baith merciless.

Taen-up aa wi my affairs,
what I maun spend, what I maun hain,
I saw throu the black shiny pane;
he tuik me geynear unawares.

I see him, by the winnock-bar,
yerkan his heid as I yerk mine;
luik maikan luik in double line,
ilk of the ither is made war.

Yon luik has flasht frae my faither's een
in Edinbrugh, and hou faur hyne
in Sutherland, and hou lang syne
in Stromness, Dornoch, Aberdeen?

I beik about my cosy, bricht,
fluorescent electric warld.
He sees me yet, yon norland yarl;
I steik my shutters guid and ticht.

ROBERT GARIOCH (1909–81)

mirk – dark; *hain* – save; *geynear* – almost; *winnock* – window;
war – aware; *hyne* – back; *beik* – warm myself; *steik* – close

To Alexander Graham

Lying asleep walking
Last night I met my father
Who seemed pleased to see me.
He wanted to speak. I saw
His mouth saying something
But the dream had no sound.

We were surrounded by
Laid-up paddle steamers
In The Old Quay in Greenock.
I smelt the tar and the ropes.

It seemed that I was standing
Beside the big iron cannon
The tugs used to tie up to
When I was a boy. I turned
To see Dad standing just
Across the causeway under
That one lamp they keep on.

He recognised me immediately.
I could see that. He was
The handsome, same age
With his good brows as when
he would take me on Sundays
Saying we'll go for a walk.

Dad, what am I doing here?
What is it I am doing now?
Are you proud of me?
Going away, I knew
You wanted to tell me something.

You stopped and almost turned back
To say something. My father,
I try to be the best
In you you give me always.

Lying asleep turning
Round in the quay-lit dark
It was my father standing
As real as life. I smelt
The quay's tar and the ropes.

I think he wanted to speak.
But the dream had no sound.
I think I must have loved him.

W. S. GRAHAM (1918–86)

Inquisition

The interviewer asks me about
'your homosexuality'
as if it were a mildly embarrassing
essential adjunct I carry
like a colostomy bag.

The interviewer asks me
'what your father would have
thought of it had he lived?'
when I know he knew,

dodged it every time he looked at me
because I was a mirror
and mourn him every day
because he died before he ever got to know me.

DAVID KINLOCH (b.1959)

Fathers and Sons

I remember being ashamed of my father
when he whispered the words out loud
reading the newspaper.

'Don't you find
the use of phonetic urban dialect
rather constrictive?'
asks a member of the audience.

The poetry reading is over.
I will go home to my children.

TOM LEONARD (b.1944)

At My Father's Grave

The sunlicht still on me, you row'd in clood,
We look upon each ither noo like hills
Across a valley. I'm nae mair your son.
It is my mind, nae son o' yours, that looks,
And the great darkness o' your death comes up
And equals it across the way.
A livin' man upon a deid man thinks
And ony sma'er thocht's impossible.

HUGH MacDIARMID (1892–1978)

row'd – wrapped

Not a Day

I wanted to write not a day
will go past when you won't
think of your father – your body
older by years now than his was.
Crossing the park under grey skies
maybe for morning rolls it seems
you are walking to meet him

Not invariably true but even a day
when you think he did not cross
your mind you think now possibly
yes – only his thought escaped you.
He is around here often like the trees
up on that slope standing on tiptoe
to follow the fate of a rain cloud
over each other's shoulders.

Water in the pond this morning
has camouflaged itself as clay.
Moorhens scratch rules in cuneiform
from a survival book of reed-running.
Their vees of ripples
soon slip back into smooth opaque.
Fathers or mothers pushing go-chairs
bring toddlers to the edge to look –
ducklings and chicks at swim.

Who kick both legs together
rattling their buggies in delight.
I pass them by – just some old guy
of indeterminate age with a grey
beard but still looking not too bad
considering in these Original chinos
with the expanding waistband
'built for durability and comfort'.

JAMES McGONIGAL (b.1947)

Ailsa Craig

It bulked large above my sandcastles:
a stepping-stone from a land of giants,
with a noose of surf around its neck.

One blustery sunset, turning purple,
it reared above my father's head
as he slammed outdoors from a row,

to sulk on the fuming causeway.
Geysers of spume were spouting high
as he strode down past the warning-signs,

and the last light was a hellish red
as he dwindled, stooping, into the rocks,
and drowned in my streaming eyes.

He'll be right back, my mother said.
But I saw the Irish Sea overwhelm
a rage that could shake a tenement.

He'd never looked so small, and wrong.
I never knew what drove him there,
but I saw him thrashed by a stormy God,

and he never seemed so tall again.
I'd never seen him so whole, before
I saw that tombstone over his head.

GERALD MANGAN (b.1951)

The Fathers

Our fathers all were poor,
Poorer our fathers' fathers;
Beyond, we dare not look.
We, the sons, keep store
Of tarnished gold that gathers
Around us from the night,
Record it in this book
That, when the line is drawn,
Credit and creditor gone,
Column and figure flown,
Will open into light.

Archaic fevers shake
Our healthy flesh and blood
Plumped in the passing day
And fed with pleasant food.
The fathers' anger and ache
Will not, will not away
And leave the living alone,
But on our careless brows
Faintly their furrows engrave
Like veinings in a stone,
Breathe in the sunny house
Nightmare of blackened bone,
Cellar and choking cave.

Panics and furies fly
Through our unhurried veins,
Heavenly lights and rains
Purify heart and eye,
Past agonies purify
And lay the sullen dust.
The angers will not away.
We hold our fathers' trust,
Wrong, riches, sorrow and all
Until they topple and fall,
And fallen let in the day.

EDWIN MUIR (1887–1959)

A Letter from My Father

It's extant only on official forms –
the wee coiled writing of my father.

His copperplate chalked on corporation
slate was lyric, legible, neat.

On tax returns its furls and curlicues
were daintier far than *Carolingian Minuscule*.

Yet he hated writing and many's the chit
or docket I penned for him

in the naïve scrawl that prints these lines.
Through all my journeyings, small triumphs

and reverses
I never had a note from him; whatever

needed telling, he was more inclined to say.
Slicing through the post these mornings

how I crave a letter from my father,
paternal greetings in a flawless script.

DONNY O'ROURKE (b.1959)

In Memoriam: My Father
(29 April, 1944)

Shut in his frosty valley at the Northern fringe of time,
Beyond the tundra and the ever-howling wolves,
The hours went slowly by, the minutes knocking lame,
As sixty summers lay counted on his shelves.

A life ebbed slowly down the Solway of its years,
Forgetting the floods of youth, the tides that swept
More cruel in their intensity than all the heartfelt tears
Which stained the linen pillow on which the dreamer slept.

The lock-gates of the life he always loved
Could still withstand the batterings of disease,
Despite Death's mathematics which had often proved
Himself the one physician to bring perfect ease.

Now I, lying all these hundred miles to the south,
Can think of him dispassionately, with pity;
Recalling tonight the weak but usually kindly mouth,
The mind that shuddered from the world's immensity;

Recalling the man whose universe was sometimes shut
Within the unmeasured boundaries of a postage-stamp;
The man for whom the mellow whisky could garotte
The marchers of history with their metronomic tramp;

The man who built as strong as man could build
Yet saw, before his end, how bricks and concrete fell away
As the destiny he always feared was finally fulfilled
And all the horror of his youth again held sway.

This man, as complex as an antique clock,
Was my own father whom I cannot see quite round;
I work all night and yet my portraits lack
Those final touches which would show I understand

The man as man, divorced from being only me,
Copying my own image in an eternal mirror:
The facts which others now report can only be
The distortions caused by my inevitable error.

When last I saw him, lying uneasy on his bed,
I knew that I at length had grown to be a man,
For all my rancours and my fears were dead;
I saw him once again as when my memory began.

And it is thus I hope I will remember him;
Before his share of the world's apple proved too sour,
Before his dreams of greatness loomed too dim
In the haze which helped to pass the intolerable hour.

I would remember him as the man who drew
With coloured chalks upon my childhood's page,
The witch from whom no small boy ever flew,
The friendly troll, the ogre who had hardly any rage.

So to his memory, I dedicate these lines,
Dumb with a feeling I cannot now express;
Glad that, at least, the heartache which remains
Instead of hating has learned how to bless.

RUTHVEN TODD (1914–78)

A letter from

A letter from a dead man,
what urgence could that lend?
which starts:
    'Received yours . . .
thanks for all the news . . .
and wishes . . . too bad that . . . '

Nothing significant
beyond what he might intend?
going on:
    'We're pleased . . .
the parcel safely . . . so in due time,
all does arrive . . . I had the . . . '

Written while still alive,
so why hope it could portend
to more than:
    'Our recent news is . . .
came and went . . . our plans are . . .
no space for more . . . it's sad that . . . '?

A letter from a dead man,
how could I want that it should end?
which does:
    'Now having autumn sunshine
mixed with cold . . . We're glad that . . .
greet everyone there for us . . .
all our love . . . Dad.'

GAEL TURNBULL (1928–2004)

A Poet's Welcome

to his love-begotten Daughter; the first instance that
entitled him to the venerable appellation of Father –

Thou's welcome, Wean! Mischanter fa' me,
If thoughts o' thee, or yet thy Mamie,
Shall ever daunton me or awe me,
           My bonie lady;
Or if I blush when thou shalt ca' me
              Tyta, or Daddie. –

Tho' now they ca' me, Fornicator,
And tease my name in kintra clatter,
The mair they talk, I'm kend the better;
           E'en let them clash!
An auld wife's tongue's a feckless matter
           To gie ane fash. –

Welcome! My bonie, sweet, wee Dochter!
Tho' ye come here a wee unsought for;
And tho' your comin I hae fought for,
           Baith Kirk and Queir;
Yet by my faith, ye're no unwrought for,
           That I shall swear!

Wee image o' my bonie Betty,
As fatherly I kiss and daut thee,
As dear and near my heart I set thee,
           Wi' as gude will,
As a' the Priests had seen me get thee
           That's out o' h—. –

Sweet fruit o' monie a merry dint,
My funny toil is no a' tint;
Tho' ye come to the warld asklent,
                    Which fools may scoff at,
In my last plack your part's be in 't,
                    The better half o't. –

Tho' I should be the waur bestead,
Thou's be as braw and bienly clad,
And thy young years as nicely bred
                    Wi' education,
As any brat o' Wedlock's bed,
                    In a' thy station. –

Lord grant that thou may ay inherit,
Thy Mither's looks an' gracefu' merit;
An' thy poor, worthless Daddie's spirit,
                    Without his failins!
'Twad please me mair to see thee heir it
                    Than stocked mailins!

For if thou be, what I wad hae thee,
And tak the counsel I shall gie thee,
I'll never rue my trouble wi' thee,
                    The cost nor shame o't,
But be a loving Father to thee,
                    And brag the name o't. –

ROBERT BURNS (1759–1796)

mischanter – misadventure; *daunton* – discourage; *clash* – gossip;
fash – bother; *daut* – fondle; *dint* – chance, occasion; *tint* – lost;
asklent – askew, on the side; *plack* – farthing, worthless coin;
mailins – farms

Mons Meg

for my daughter

Under warmed, antiseasonal skies
Zoo capercailzies flap away

Towards the terminus of species;
Headsetted tourists evolve into

Cyborgs on the Castle ramparts;
But I have ears and eyes only for you,

Wee ballerina, pas-de-bas-ing in front of Mons Meg,
Singing down the barrel of that gun.

I love how you yell a pirouette,
'Hullo, Mons Meg! Goodbye, Mons Meg!'

Blithe beside its heavy, pitch-black muzzle,
Laughing in the cannon's mouth.

ROBERT CRAWFORD (b.1959)

from **A Bard's Address to His Youngest Daughter**

Come to my arms my wee wee pet
My mild my blithesome Harriet
The sweetest babe art thou to me
That ever sat on parent's knee.
Thou hast that eye was mine erewhile
Thy mother's blithe and grateful smile
And such a playful merry vein
That greybeards smile at pranks of thine

And if aright I read thy mind
The child of nature thou'rt designed
For even while yet upon the breast
Thou mimic'st child and bird and beast
Can'st cry like Moggy o'er her book
And crow like cock and caw like rook
Boo like a bull and blare like ram
And bark like dog and bleat like lamb
And when abroad in pleasant weather
Thou minglest all these sounds together
Then who can say, thou happy creature,
Thou'rt not the very child of nature

*

How dar'st thou frown, thou freakish fay,
And pout and look the other way?
Why turn thy chubby cheeks athraw

And skelp the beard of thy papa?
I know full well thy deep design
'Tis to turn back thine eye on mine
With triple burst of joyful glee
And fifty strains at mimicry
What wealth from nature may'st thou won
With pupilage so soon begun.
Well, hope is all; thou art unproved,
The bard's and nature's best beloved.
And now above thy brow so fair
And flowing films of flaxen hair
I lay my hand once more and frame
A blessing in the holy name
Of that supreme divinity
Who breathed a living soul in thee

JAMES HOGG (1770–1835)

At First, My Daughter

She is world without understanding.
She is made of sound.
She drinks me.

We laugh when I lift her by the feet.
She is new as a petal.
Water comes out of her mouth and her little crotch.

She gives the crook of my arm
A weight of delight.
I stare in her moving mirror of untouched flesh.

Absurd, but verifiable,
These words – mother, daughter –
They taste of receiving and relinquishing.

She will never again be quite so novel and lovely
Nor I so astonished.
In touch, we are celebrating

The first and last moments
Of being together and separate
Indissolute – till we are split

By time, and growth, and man,
The things I made her with.

ELMA MITCHELL (1919–2000)

The world is busy, Katie

The world is busy, Katie, and tonight
the planes are playing, fine, alright, but soon
the folk behind those blinks will nap, sleep tight,
as you will too, beneath a nitelite moon.
The world is busy, Katie, but it's late –
the trains are packing up, the drunks are calm.
The fast, the slow, has gone. It's only freight
that storms the garage lane. It means no harm.
The world is busy, Katie, but it's dark –
the lorries nod, they snort, they spoil their chrome.
They hate to be alone. For them, a lay-by's home.
The world is busy, Katie, like I said,
but *you're* the world – and tired. It's time for bed.

RICHARD PRICE (b.1966)

To My Son

Those flaxen locks, those eyes of blue,
Bright as thy mother's in their hue;
Those rosy lips, whose dimples play
And smile to steal the heart away,
Recall a scene of former joy,
And touch thy father's heart, my Boy!

And thou canst lisp a father's name –
Ah, William, were thine own the same, –
No self-reproach – but, let me cease –
My care for thee shall purchase peace;
Thy mother's shade shall smile in joy,
And pardon all the past, my Boy!

Her lowly grave the turf has prest,
And thou hast known a stranger's breast;
Derision sneers upon thy birth,
And yields thee scarce a name on earth;
Yet shall not these one hope destroy, –
A father's heart is thine, my Boy!

Why, let the world unfeeling frown,
Must I fond Nature's claim disown
Ah, no – though moralists reprove,
I hail thee, dearest child of love,
Fair cherub, pledge of youth and joy –
A father guards thy birth, my Boy!

Oh, 'twill be sweet in thee to trace,
Ere age has wrinkled o'er my face,
Ere half my glass of life is run,
At once a brother and a son;
And all my wane of years employ
In justice done to thee, my Boy!

Although so young thy heedless sire,
Youth will not damp parental fire;
And, wert thou still less dear to me,
While Helen's form revives in thee,
The breast, which beat to former joy,
Will ne'er desert its pledge, my Boy!

GEORGE GORDON, LORD BYRON (1788–1824)

Blue Een

Blue een,
What ha'e ye dune wi' my laddie?
Ye ha'e stolen his he'rt awa'
Frae me, his mither.
Blue een,
I did the same wi' his daddie,
Sae fine I ken the look
That ye gi'e each ither.

Blue een,
At your tryst in the mirk the nicht
Were your een like staurs,
Wi' the licht o' love alowe,
That he could but look at ye, lass,
An' haud ye ticht,
As his daddie did when he gi'ed me
The same auld vow?

Gin I greet, lass,
It's no' that I'm sad;
I gi'e him tae ye gladly
Wi'oot a swither.
Ye ha'e true een:
Gin ye're guid tae my lad,
He'll never ken what it is
Tae miss his mither.

W. D. COCKER (1882–1970)

mirk – dark; *alowe* – on fire; *swither* – hesitation

Growing Up

On Sundays I would take the boys to play
in Holyrood Park (we once had to knock
on the Palace door and ask for our ball back).
At that age the competitive spirit was high:

they'd fly into the tackle hell-for-leather
till I'd warn, 'Any more fouls of that kind,
we're off home', then have to stick to my guns
or lose face (*hoist* and *petard* come to mind).

Was this instilling a sense of fair play,
or simple abuse of power? I remember
the small group trudging back to the car,
the sullen silence throughout the journey.

Six-footers now, they're able to cope
with life's greater buffetings, take mature
decisions affecting themselves and others.
But I wonder, did their father ever grow up?

STEWART CONN (b.1936)

The Tay Moses

What can I fashion
for you but a woven
creel of river-
rashes, a golden
oriole's nest, my gift
wrought from the Firth –

and choose my tide: either
the flow, when, watertight
you'll drift to the uplands –
my favourite hills; held safe
in eddies, where salmon, wisdom
and guts withered in spawn,
rest between moves – that
slither of body as you were born –

or the ebb, when the water
will birl you to snag
on reeds, the river-
pilot leaning over the side:
'*Name o God!*' and you'll change hands:
tractor-man, grieve, farm-wife
who takes you into her
competent arms

even as I drive, slamming
the car's gears,

spitting gravel on tracks
down between berry-fields,
engine still racing, the door wide
as I run toward her, crying
LEAVE HIM! Please,
it's okay, he's mine.

KATHLEEN JAMIE (b.1962)

The Wonderfu' Wean

Our wean's the most wonderfu' wean e'er I saw,
It would tak' me a lang summer day to tell a'
His pranks, frae the morning till night shuts his e'e,
When he sleeps like a peerie, 'tween father and me.
For in his quiet turns, siccan questions he'll speir:
How the moon can stick up in the sky that's sae clear?
What gars the wind blaw? and wharfrae comes the rain?
He's a perfect divert: he's a wonderfu' wean!

Or wha was the first body's father? and wha
Made the very first snaw-shower that ever did fa'?
And wha made the first bird that sang on a tree?
And the water that sooms a' the ships on the sea? –
But after I've tell't him as weel as I ken,
Again he begins wi' his 'Wha?' and his 'When?'
And he looks aye sae watchfu' the while I explain, –
He's as auld as the hills – he's an auld-farrant wean.

And folk wha ha'e skill o' the lumps on the head,
Hint there's mae ways than toiling o' winning ane's bread;
How he'll be a rich man, and ha'e men to work for him,
Wi' a kyte like a bailie's, shug-shugging afore him,
Wi' a face like the moon, sober, sonsy, and douce,
And a back, for its breadth, like the side o' a house.
'Tweel I'm unco tae'en up wi't, they mak' a' sae plain, –
He's just a town's talk – he's a by-ord'nar wean!

I ne'er can forget sic a laugh as I gat,
When I saw him put on his father's waistcoat and hat;
Then the lang-leggit boots gaed sae far owre his knees,
The tap loops wi' his fingers he grippit wi' ease,
Then he march'd thro' the house, he march'd but,
                                                he march'd ben,
That I leugh clean outright, for I couldna contain,
He was sic a conceit – sic an ancient-like wean.

But 'mid a' his daffin' sic kindness he shows,
That he's dear to my heart as the dew to the rose;
And the unclouded hinnie-beam aye in his e'e,
Mak's him every day dearer and dearer to me.
Though fortune be saucy, and dorty, and dour,
And glooms through her fingers, like hills through a shower,
When bodies hae got ae bit bairn o' their ain,
How he cheers up their hearts, – he's the wonderfu' wean.

WILLIAM MILLER (1810–72)

peerie – top; *speir* – ask; *auld farrant* – with the wisdom of older folk;
kyte – stomach; *dorty* – haughty

The Thread

James made his landing in the world
so hard he ploughed straight back into the earth.
They caught him by the thread of his one breath
and pulled him up. They don't know how it held.
And so today I thank what higher will
brought us to here, to you and me and Russ,
the great twin-engined swaying wingspan of us
roaring down the back of Kirrie Hill

and your two-year-old lungs somehow out-revving
every engine in the universe.
All that trouble just to turn up dead
was all I thought that long week. Now the thread
is holding all of us: look at our tiny house,
son, the white dot of your mother waving.

DON PATERSON (b.1963)

Daedalus

My son has birds in his head.

I know them now. I catch
the pitch of their calls, their shrill
cacophonies, their chitterings, their coos.
They hover behind his eyes and come to rest
on a branch, on a book, grow still,
claws curled, wings furled.
His is a bird world.

I learn the flutter of his moods,
his moments of swoop and soar.
From the ground I feel him try
the limits of the air –
sudden lift, sudden terror –
and move in time to cradle
his quivering, feathered fear.

At evening, in the tower,
I see him to sleep and see
the hooding-over of eyes,
the slow folding of wings.
I wake to his morning twitterings,
to the *croomb* of his becoming.

He chooses his selves – wren, hawk,
swallow or owl – to explore
the trees and rooftops of his heady wishing.
Tomtit, birdwit.
Am I to call him down, to give him
a grounding, teach him gravity?
Gently, gently.
Time tells us what we weigh, and soon enough
his feet will reach the ground.
Age, like a cage, will enclose him.
So the wise men said.

My son has birds in his head.

ALASTAIR REID (b.1926)

Brothers

Once, I slept in a bed with these four men who share
an older face and can be made to laugh, even now,
at random quotes from the play we were in. *There's no way
in the creation of God's earth*, I say. They grin and nod.

What was possible retreats and shrinks, and in my other eyes
they shrink to an altar boy, a boy practising scales,
a boy playing tennis with a wall, a baby
crying in the night like a new sound flailing for a shape.

Occasionally, when people ask, I enjoy reciting their names.
I don't have photographs, but I like to repeat the names.
My mother chose them. I hear her life in the words,
the breeding words, the word that broke her heart.

Much in common, me, with thieves and businessmen,
fathers and UB40s. We have nothing to say of now,
but time owns us. How tall they have grown. One day
I shall pay for a box and watch them shoulder it.

CAROL ANN DUFFY (b.1955)

Catching up with Fergus

I was nineteen when you were born.
Waiting for you shortened that first scary
winter term away from home.
I saw you only hours old, my little brother,
two weeks late; wrinkled skin, big feet.

Now it's me that's running late. I catch up
with you at six, but find you've just turned eight.
I've tracked your growing up, my distant boy,
but not come close to making out
your boy things, your reserve.
Just the other day you caught me watching.
'What?' you growled. And to my questions
answered 'stuff', 'dunno' and 's'alright'.
I sneaked around your room in school time
compiled a list, to find you in the way your 'stuff'
fits together. But I'm no nearer.

I nose through memories, make another list:
At two you pulled off all my castor-oil plant's leaves.
At five I taught you 'Three Blind Mice' on lettered piano keys.
(Now one finger drums the tune to 'Mission Impossible').
I've brushed your teeth, had baths with you. Read you stories.
Pushed you in your pram, on the swing, on your bike.
Carried you on my shoulders, on my back, in my arms.
I've written four poems about you
and known you for ten years.
When I visit, you say (but not to me) you want me to stay.
Goodbye is standing on each other's feet.

KATE HENDRY (b.1970)

The Brothers

Last night I watched my brothers play,
The gentle and the reckless one,
In a field two yards away.
For half a century they were gone
Beyond the other side of care
To be among the peaceful dead.

Even in a dream how could I dare
Interrogate that happiness
So wildly spent yet never less?
For still they raced about the green
And were like two revolving suns;
A brightness poured from head to head,
So strong I could not see their eyes
Or look into their paradise.
What were they doing, the happy ones?
Yet where I was they once had been.

I thought, How could I be so dull,
Twenty thousand days ago,
Not to see they were beautiful?
I asked them, Were you really so
As you are now, that other day?
And the dream was soon away.

For then we played for victory
And not to make each other glad.
A darkness covered every head,

Frowns twisted the original face,
And through that mask we could not see
The beauty and the buried grace.

I have observed in foolish awe
The dateless mid-days of the law
And seen indifferent justice done
By everyone on everyone.
And in a vision I have seen
My brothers playing on the green.

EDWIN MUIR (1887–1959)

The Family Contrast

O Sirs! was e'er sic difference seen
    As 'twixt wee Will and Tam?
The ane's a perfect ettercap,
    The ither's just a lamb;
Will greets and girns the lee-lang day,
    And carps at a' he gets –
Wi' ither bairns he winna play,
    But sits alane and frets.

He flings his piece into the fire,
    He yaumers at his brose,
And wae betide the luckless flee
    That lights upon his nose!
He kicks the collie, cuffs the cat,
    The hens and birds he stanes –
Na, little brat! he tak's a preen
    And jags the very weans.

Wi' spite he tumbles aff his stool,
    And there he sprawling lies,
And at his mither thraws his gab,
    Gin she but bid him rise.
Is there in a' the world beside
    Sae wild a wight as he?
Weel! gin the creature grow a man
    I wonder what he'll be!

But Tammy's just as sweet a bairn
    As ane could wish to see,
The smile aye plays around his lips,
    While blythely blinks his e'e;
He never whimpers, greets, nor girns,
    Even for a broken tae,
But rins and gets it buckled up,
    Syne out again to play.

He claps the collie, dauts the cat,
    Flings moolins to the doos,
To Bess and Bruckie rins for grass,
    To cool their honest mou's;
He's kind to ilka living thing,
    He winna hurt a flee,
And, gin he meet a beggar bairn,
    His piece he'll freely gi'e.

He tries to please wee crabbit Will,
    When in his cankriest mood,
He gi'es him a' his taps and bools,
    And tells him to be good.
Sae good a wean as oor wee Tam
    It cheers the heart to see –
O! gin his brither were like him,
    How happy might we be!

ALEXANDER RODGER (1784–1846)

ettercap – pest; *preen* – pin; *moolins* – crumbs; *doos* – pigeons;
crabbit – grumpy

Counting Out Rhyme

Seven bonnie sisters on an isle in the west:
The youngest was the fairest, and she was loved the best.

Seven wistful sisters hankering tae wed:
On the beach the mocking waves cast up a sailor dead.

The eldest, as she lugged him from the waves whaur they ran,
Said, 'A drooned man is better than nae living man.

For a reel i' the munelicht his banes will be braw;
We'll dance hot taegither while his flesh rots awa.'

Six sisters racing, till a boat it was sunk:
The waves cast up a boozing man, reeking, roudy drunk.

Five sisters hustled back, the sixth chose tae bide.
'A brawl, and a buffet, a black eye for a bride!
But a boozing man is better than nae man at my side.'

Five siren sisters vividly aflame:
The surges brought a greedy man, he gobbled as he came;

His tusks fast crunching on a muckle fish-tail.
The fifth sister grumbled, 'He's as huge as a whale!

He gorges wi' a gusto that is daunting indeed,
But a greedy man is better than nae man tae feed.'

Rough waves sprachaling, a man plunging through:
He gripped the fourth sister, and beat her black and blue.

The fourth sobbed, 'A cruel man clouts me tae my knees,
But a cruel man is better than nae man tae please.'

Three hopeful sisters turning towards the foam:
There came a dull man floating in, as if he floated home.

The third sighed, 'A dull man will haver and prate.
He'll harp and carp and din my ear, early and late.
But a dull man is better than nae man tae hate.'

Twa bonnie sisters naked in the night,
The cauld waves breaking, the mune shining bright.

The cauld waves breaking, the surf drenching doun:
It rolled in a mucky man on sands like the mune.

He was crusted thick wi' barnacles, tarry from the sea.
He scarted, and he scratched, and he girned in a gree.

'He's mucky as a tousled tyke!' the second sister said.
'But a mucky man is better than nae man in my bed.'

The youngest and the fairest, she was alone,
The first star flickering, the seagulls flown.

'A dull man, a dirty man, a drunk man,' she said,
'A cruel man, a greedy man, or a drooned man in my bed?

The sea waves may dunk them deep, for I'd refuse them a'.
I'll live alane, and happily, and love nae man at a'.'

The cats o' the kirk-yard drifted tae her side.
The hither and thither cats cam' wi' her tae bide.

Wi' cats hurra-purrying and fish swimming slaw
She lived as light-hearted as the sea-breezes blaw.

The waves broke around her wi' a rush and a roar.
They shone in the munelicht but cast nae man ashore.
By sunlicht, and munelicht, they cast nae man ashore.

One sister walking neath a weird sickle mune:
The waves phosphorescent, the night clear as noon.

A long wave lifting, it birreled as it broke.
The spray frae its flying brow went up like altar smoke.

Then cam' the unicorn, brichter than the mune,
Prancing frae the wave wi' his braw crystal croon.

Up the crisp and shelly strand he trotted unafraid.
Agin' the lanesome lassie's knee his comely head he laid.

Upon the youngest sister's lap he leaned his royal head.
She stabbed him tae the hert, and Oh! how eagerly he bled!

He died triumphant and content, his horn agin' her knee.
The crescent mune fled doun tae meet the phosphorescent sea.

'Seven!' yowled the kirk-yard cats. 'Seven!' thrummed
                                        the breeze.
'Seven!' sang the fish o' yon seraphic seas.

'Seven doomed sisters on an isle in the west:
The youngest was the fairest, and she was loved the best.'

HELEN ADAM (1909–93)

The Blue Jacket

When there comes a flower to the stingless nettle,
    To the hazel bushes, bees,
I think I can see my little sister
    Rocking herself by the hazel trees.

Rocking her arms for very pleasure
    That every leaf so sweet can smell,
And that she has on her the warm blue jacket
    Of mine, she liked so well.

Oh to win near you, little sister!
    To hear your soft lips say –
'I'll never tak' up wi' lads or lovers,
    But a baby I maun hae.

'A baby in a cradle rocking,
    Like a nut, in a hazel shell,
And a new blue jacket, like this o' Annie's,
    It sets me aye sae well.'

MARION ANGUS (1854–1944)

Sisters

Even when she moved
five hundred miles away
telepathy was alive between them
and love as strong as ever

She sends in the post
pressed tulip petals
slivers of shell from the day at the beach
wrapped in tissue paper

She, a book of stories
golden earrings

and she, the painting of a windy day
the daffodil bowl

Even before the letter
saying, between the lines, 'come',
she is on her way

ELIZABETH BURNS (b.1957)

Poem For My Sister

My little sister likes to try my shoes,
to strut in them,
admire her spindle-thin twelve-year-old legs
in this season's styles.
She says they fit her perfectly,
but wobbles
on their high heels, they're
hard to balance.

I like to watch my little sister
playing hopscotch, admire the neat hops-and-skips of her,
their quick peck,
never-missing their mark, not
over-stepping the line.
She is competent at peever.

I try to warn my little sister
about unsuitable shoes,
point out my own distorted feet, the callouses,
odd patches of hard skin.
I should not like to see her
in my shoes.
I wish she would stay
sure footed,
                sensibly shod.

LIZ LOCHHEAD (b.1947)

Yarbent
i m my Aunt Ella

You took time ta mak sure I'd gotten
ivery tirl, ivery whenk o da wird
you'd used: dat een I'd aksed aboot.
Sic an owld wird hit soonded: 'yarbent'.

I can still see you luik ta Mousa, say
'Weel, hit's a boo o wadder fae da sooth-aest,
laid on herd an dry, no lik ta shift,
maybe roond voar, or eftir hairst.'

Der a yarbent settled apön me fae you gud:
sic a peerie wird, but nirse. A'll varg
i da face o him, an keep i da mind's eye,
as you wir wint tae, da bigger pictir.

CHRISTINE DE LUCA (b.1947)

yarbent – spell of cold, dry weather; *tirl* – turn;
whenk – odd movement; *dat* – that; *hit* – it; *ta* – towards;
boo o wadder – spell of similar weather; *voar* – springtime;
hairst – harvest; *der a* – there's a; *gud* – went; *peerie* – small;
nirse – bitter; *varg* – work in difficult conditions;
wir wint tae – were accustomed to

A Tribute to Aunts

As she stands at the bedroom window
    Aunt Mabel carefully tilts
her perfectly-coiffured head, and reconnoitres
    the seascape below.
Parents in sepia, a cousin, smiling friends
    stand loyally at her elbow
in their ranks of little silver frames.
    All dispositions are intact.
There is no reason to be anxious, it seems.

    Over her shoulder a sunbeam
picks out a glint of dancing specks.
    There is tomorrow's enemy
when twice she will dust the Victorian sampler,
    adjust the watercolour
from a celebrated artist (memento perhaps
    of more than friendship).
Studiously she will attend to the deployment
    of doilies on coffee-tables,
ensure the decorum of every chair and curtain fold,
    each sacred bibelot,
for her creed is comprehensive and precise.

This is not my country, for I still keep in an attic
    a shawl-wrapped ghost
rocking, rocking in a God-intoxicated trance,

and rarely can I forget
the Protestant passion for invisible light.
   But her frontiers are different,
and I salute the courage of aunts who live
   in the piety of order,
bravely maintaining the barricades
   against Chaos and old Night
behind a row of Capo da Monte figurines.

NORMAN KREITMAN (b.1927)

Aunt Julia

Aunt Julia spoke Gaelic
very loud and very fast.
I could not answer her –
I could not understand her.

She wore men's boots
when she wore any.
– I can see her strong foot,
stained with peat,
paddling with the treadle of the spinningwheel
while her right hand drew yarn
marvellously out of the air.

Hers was the only house
where I've lain at night
in the absolute darkness
of a box bed, listening to
crickets being friendly.

She was buckets
and water flouncing into them.
She was winds pouring wetly
round house-ends.
She was brown eggs, black skirts
and a keeper of threepennybits
in a teapot.

Aunt Julia spoke Gaelic
very loud and very fast.
By the time I had learned
a little, she lay
silenced in the absolute black
of a sandy grave
at Luskentyre.
But I hear her still, welcoming me
with a seagull's voice
across a hundred yards
of peatscapes and lazybeds
and getting angry, getting angry
with so many questions
unanswered.

NORMAN MacCAIG (1910–96)

Aunt Myra (1901–1989)

A horse in a field in a picture is easy.
A man in a room with a fan, we wonder.
It might be whirring blades in steamy downtown –
but no, it's what she's left beside her dance-cards.
How she sat out a foxtrot at the Plaza
and fanned her brow, those far-off flirty Twenties
he opens and shuts with an unpractised gesture
that leaves the years half-laughing at the pathos
of the clumsy, until rising strings have swept them
dancing again into silence. The room darkens
with a blue lingering glow above the roof-tops
but the man still stands there, holding up the dangling
dance-cards by their tiny attached pencils.
The cords which are so light seem to him heavy
as if they were about to take the strain of
tender evenings descending into memory.
Something is hard, not easy, though it's clearly
a man, a fan, a woman, a room, a picture.

EDWIN MORGAN (b.1920)

Great Aunt

Now scarcely
brought to mind
for thirty years
with whom I shared

five summer days
'ganging the roon'
your kin and mine
through the Borders,

Lanark, Lothian,
drunk with mostly
not much sleep
and tea and talk,

such talk
'guid crack'
as if excess
were timeless:

as chauffeur,
almost grandson,
briefly confidant
of you, my dear,

and even then
long widowed,
now long dead
great aunt,

here suddenly
in the particular
lift of a chin,
bob of a throat,

step of a girl
crossing the street
to meet her friends
this winter afternoon.

GAEL TURNBULL (1928–2004)

Forebears

My father's uncle was the fastest
thing on two wheels, sitting in a gig,
the reins tight, his back at an angle
of thirty degrees, puffing up dust-clouds
as he careered down Craigie Hill.

His father before him, the strongest man
in Ayrshire, took a pair of cartwheels
by the axle and walked off with them: I have
visions of him in the meadow, holding
two ropes, a stallion straining on each.

Before that, no doubt, we boasted
the straightest furrow, the richest yield.
No measurements needed: each farm
bore its best, as each tree its fruit.
We even had a crazy creature in crinolines

who locked her letters in a brass box.
Others too . . . but what do such truths
add up to – when the nearest
(and furthest) I get is visiting
their elaborately cared-for graves?

On an adjoining stone are a skull
and hourglass, from Covenanter
days. Their lives a duller
sacrifice. John on his moral staff,

the great-aunts with their rigid ways,

smacking of goodness in the strictest
sense, members of a sect, Elect almost,
shared surely something of flint
in the brain: their mortal goal
salvation, through purification of the soul.

STEWART CONN (b.1936)

Uncle Roderick

His drifter swung in the night
from a mile of nets
between the Shiants and Harris.

My boy's eyes watched
the lights of the fishing fleet – fireflies
on the green field of the sea.

In the foc's'le he gave me a bowl
of tea, black, strong and bitter,
and a biscuit you hammered
in bits like a plate.

The fiery curtain came up
from the blackness, comma'd with corpses.

Round Rhu nan Cuideagan
he steered for home, a boy's god
in seaboots. He found his anchorage
as a bird its nest.

In the kitchen he dropped
his oilskins where he stood.

He was strong as the red bull.
He moved like a dancer.
He was a cran of songs.

NORMAN MacCAIG (1910–96)

from My Canadian Uncle

1
Canada feels large and transient.
We leave Vancouver in a glittering sun,
heading for White Rock, my uncle's own
and carefully built house. We let the breeze
stream past us freshly through the open windows.
The traffic lights ahead of us hang down
at the road's centre, and we bullet on.
At 85 he's driving. He goes home
to Lewis every year, but all are dead
whom he once knew, all under white and red
flowers in the windy cemetery. He sits
crag-faced and tanned, short-sleeved, and beats the lights
with mischievous relish.

                                    Canada extends
from Vancouver northwards: to where once he saw
black bears chew berries on a calm cool day.
'Old son,' they told him at the station, 'You
may drive the month your visitors are here.
But after that . . . '

                                      'I'll tell you' (in the clear
air, he says), 'You can exceed the limit
by a mile or so.' We tremble in our seats.
Impossible Canada so vast and mild.
You're not a Lewisman, you're Canada's child.
He fires his long white Plymouth at the gate,

puts on his glasses, backs out of the light
into the garage, as if he steered a boat,
gets out and says, 'Well then this is it.'
The wooden house, the garden, and the snake
basking in sunlight on his own White Rock.

4
Sitting in his garden in the sun
in my green Canadian jockey cap I dozed
below the cherries, colour of red wine.
The crows had pecked them to a rotten brown.
He had a wire strung out from the kitchen
which he would pull, to a clamour of loud cans,
which then would dance and dance and dance and dance.
A Stetson hat hung high above the garden.
He knew by sight each individual crow
so sleek and black, a devilish Free Church hue.
'Whatever we would get we would have to pay
for later. I once told a man –
from Paisley, I think it was, he was making fun
of Highlanders – I said to him one day,
"We had the best of food when I was young,
crowdie and salmon, oatcakes and fresh fish.
We lived like princes in so-called barren Lewis." '
I peered beneath the visor of my cap.
He stood beside the red and velvety rose
he'd planted for his wife. The shiny crows
were hovering round us. 'We never once
quarrelled, Mary and myself. And I composed
poems since she died. I said, No drugs.

I held her hand at the end. Here the graves
are flat, not upright. I will take you there.
Vandals steal the flowers.'

                                Later he said
'I'll bring some girls I know along for tea.'
They were seventy years old and both had sticks.
We sat in the cherry garden in the fine
monotonous sunlight. The two ladies' hands
trembled among tea cups.

                                 With a hose
he carefully watered the red Empire rose.

IAIN CRICHTON SMITH (1928–98)

English Cousin Comes to Scotland

See when my English cousin comes,
it's so embarrassing so it is, so it is.
I have to explain everything
I mean Every Thing, so I do, so I do.
I told her, 'know what happened to me?
I got skelped, because I screamed when a skelf
went into my pinky finger: OUCH, loud.
And ma ma dropped her best bit of china.
It wis sore, so it wis, so it wis.
I was scunnert being skelped
when I wis already sore.
So I ran and ran, holding
my pinky, through the park,
over the burn, up the hill.
I was knackered and I fell
into the mud and went home
mocket and got skelped again.
So I locked myself in the cludgie
and cried, so I did, so I did,
pulling the long roll of paper
onto the floor. Like that dug Andrex.'
Whilst I'm saying this, my English cousin
has her mouth open. Glaikit.
Stupit. So she is, so she is.
I says, 'I'm going to have to learn you

what's what.' And at that the wee git
cheers up; the wee toffee nose says,
'not learn you, teach you,' like she's scored.

JACKIE KAY (b.1961)

skelped – smacked; *skelf* – splinter; *scunnert* – really annoyed

To Willie and Henrietta

If two may read aright
These rhymes of old delight
And house and garden play,
You two, my cousins, and you only, may.

You in a garden green
With me were king and queen,
Were hunter, soldier, tar,
And all the thousand things that children are.

Now in the elders' seat
We rest with quiet feet,
And from the window-bay
We watch the children, our successors, play.

'Time was,' the golden head
Irrevocably said;
But time which none can bind,
While flowing fast away, leaves love behind.

ROBERT LOUIS STEVENSON (1850–94)

ACKNOWLEDGEMENTS

Our thanks are due to the following authors, publishers and estates who have generously given permission to reproduce works:

Helen Adam, 'Counting Out Rhyme' from *A Helen Adam Reader* (National Poetry Foundation 2007) reprinted by permission of The Poetry Collection, University at Buffalo; Marion Angus, 'The Blue Jacket' from *Voices from their ain Country* (ASLS 2006) reprinted by permission of Alan J Byatt; George Bruce, 'Father and the Silver Salver' from *Today Tomorrow* (Polygon 2001) reprinted by permission of Birlinn Ltd; Elizabeth Burns, 'Grandmother' from *The Lantern Bearers* (Shoestring Press 2007), and 'Sisters' from *Ophelia and other poems* (Polygon 1991) reprinted by permission of Shoestring Press and Birlinn Ltd; Ron Butlin, 'Five Years Later' from *Without a Backward Glance* (Barzan 2005) reprinted by permission of the author; Jim Carruth, 'The Field' from *Bovine Pastoral* (Ludovic Press 2004) reprinted by permission of the author; Kate Clanchy, 'My Grandfather' from *Samarkand* (Picador 1999) reprinted by permission of Pan Macmillan; W.D. Cocker, 'Blue Een' from *Dandie and other poems* (Gowans & Gray 1925) reprinted by permission of Brown, Son & Ferguson; Stewart Conn, 'Family Visit' and 'Forebears' from *Stolen Light: Selected Poems* (Bloodaxe Books 1999), and 'Growing Up' from *Ghosts at Cockcrow* (Bloodaxe Books 2005) reprinted by permission of Bloodaxe; Robert Crawford, 'Opera' from *A Scottish Assembly* (Jonathan Cape 1990) and 'Mons Meg' from *The Tip of My Tongue* (Jonathan Cape 2003) reprinted by permission of The Random House Group Ltd; Christine De Luca, 'Yarbent' from *Parallel Worlds* (Luath Press 2005) reprinted by permission of Luath Press; Carol Ann Duffy, 'Brothers' from *Mean Time* (Anvil Press 1993) reprinted by permission of Anvil Press; Gerrie Fellows, 'Photograph of My Grandparents' from *The Powerlines* (Polygon 2000) reprinted by permission of Birlinn Ltd; Alison Flett, 'Lernin' from *Whit Lassyz Ur Inty* (Thirsty Books 2004) reprinted by permission of Argyll Publishing; Robert Garioch, 'My Faither Sees Me' from *Complete Poetical Works* (Macdonald 1983) reprinted by permission of

Birlinn Ltd; W. S. Graham, 'To Alexander Graham' from *New Collected Poems* (Faber 2004) reprinted by permission of Faber and Faber Ltd; Diana Hendry, 'Grandma as a Genie' from *Borderers* (Peterloo 2001) and 'Dressing Mother' from *Making Blue* (Peterloo 1995) reprinted by permission of the author; Kate Hendry, 'Catching up with Fergus' from *Orbis* 119 (2000) reprinted by permission of the author; W.N. Herbert, 'The Harvest in March' from *The Big Bumper Book of Troy* (Bloodaxe Books 2002) reprinted by permission of Bloodaxe; Kathleen Jamie, 'Crystal Set' from *Mr & Mrs Scotland Are Dead* (Bloodaxe Books 2002) reprinted by permission of Bloodaxe, 'The Tay Moses' from *Jizzen* (Picador 1999) reprinted by permission of Pan Macmillan, London; Jackie Kay, 'The Telling Part' and 'I Kin See Richt Thru My Mither' from *Darling: New & Selected Poems* (Bloodaxe Books 2007) reprinted by permission of Bloodaxe, and 'Grandpa's Soup' from *The Frog who Dreamed she was an Opera Singer* (Bloomsbury 1998) reprinted by permission of Bloomsbury, and 'English Cousin Comes to Scotland' from *Two's Company* (Blackie 1992) reprinted by permission of the author; David Kinloch, 'Inquisition' from *In My Father's House* (Carcanet Press 2005) reprinted by permission of Carcanet Press Ltd; Norman Kreitman, 'A Tribute to Aunts' from *Casanova's 72nd Birthday* (Akros Publications 2003) reprinted by permission of the author; Tom Leonard, 'Fathers and Sons' from *Intimate Voices* (Galloping Dog Press 1984) reprinted by permission of the author; Liz Lochhead, 'For My Grandmother Knitting' and 'Poem for My Sister' from *Dreaming Frankenstein* (Polygon 1984) and 'Sorting Through' from *The Colour of Black and White* (Polygon 2003) reprinted by permission of Birlinn Ltd; Brian McCabe, 'The Big Sister Poems' from *The Lipstick Circus* (Polygon 1987) reprinted by permission of Birlinn Ltd; Norman MacCaig, 'Grandchild', 'Aunt Julia' and 'Uncle Roderick' from *The Poems* (Polygon 2005) reprinted by permission of Birlinn Ltd; Hugh MacDiarmid, 'At My Father's Grave' from *Complete Poems* (Martin Brian & O'Keeffe 1978) reprinted by permission of Carcanet Press Ltd; James McGonigal, 'Not a day' reprinted by permission of the author; Alasdair Maclean, 'Stone' from *From the Wilderness* (Gollancz 1973) reprinted by permission of the Orion

Publishing Group, London; Robert McLellan, 'Sang' from Douglas Young, ed., *Scottish Verse 1851–1951* (Nelson 1952) reprinted by permission of John McLellan; Hugh McMillan, 'The World Book of the McMillans' from *Aphrodite's Anorak* (Peterloo Poets 1996) reprinted by permission of Peterloo Poets; Angela McSeveney, 'Be-Ro' from *Slaughtering Beetroot* (Mariscat 2008) reprinted by permission of the author; Gerald Mangan, 'Ailsa Craig' from *Waiting for the Storm* (Bloodaxe Books 1990) reprinted by permission of the author; Elma Mitchell, 'Mother, Dear Mother' and 'At First, My Daughter' from *The Human Cage* (Peterloo 1979) reprinted by permission of Peterloo Poets; Edwin Morgan, 'The Coals' from *Collected Poems* (Carcanet Press 1990) and 'Aunt Myra' from *Sweeping Out The Dark* (Carcanet Press 1994) reprinted by permission of Carcanet Press Ltd; Edwin Muir, 'Childhood', 'The Fathers' and 'The Brothers' from *Complete Poems* (ASLS 1991) reprinted by permission of Faber and Faber Ltd; Donny O'Rourke, 'Milk' and 'A Letter from my Father' from *The Waistband* (Polygon 1997) reprinted by permission of Birlinn Ltd; Don Paterson, 'The Thread' from *Landing Light* (Faber 2003) reprinted by permission of Faber and Faber Ltd; Tom Pow, 'Sleepless' from *Sparks!* (Mariscat Press 2005) reprinted by permission of the author; Richard Price, 'The World is Busy, Katie' from *Lucky Day* (Carcanet Press 2005) reprinted by permission of Carcanet Press Ltd; Pauline Prior-Pitt, 'Grand-child' from *Ironing with Sue Lawley* (Spike Press 2005) reprinted by permission of the author; Alastair Reid, 'Daedalus' from *Weathering* (Canongate 1978) reprinted by permission of the author; Iain Crichton Smith, 'You Lived in Glasgow' from *Collected Poems* (Carcanet Press 1992) and 'My Canadian Uncle' from *A Country for Old Men & My Canadian Uncle* (Carcanet Press 2000) reprinted by permission of Carcanet Press Ltd; Ruthven Todd, 'In Memoriam: My Father' from *Garland for the Winter Solstice* (Little Brown 1961) reprinted by permission of David Higham Associates; Gael Turnbull, 'Great Aunt' and 'A Letter from' from *There Are Words: Collected Poems* (Shearsman Press, in association with Mariscat Press) reprinted by permission of Jill Turnbull.